WORLD BANK STAFF OCCASIONAL PAPERS □ NUMBER TWENTY-FOUR

Syamaprasad Gupta

A Model for Income Distribution, Employment, and Growth

A Case Study of Indonesia

assisted by Ellen Andersson and Ronald Padula

Published for the World Bank
The Johns Hopkins University Press
Baltimore and London

Manufactured in the United States of America.

The views and interpretations in this book are those of the author and should not be attributed to the World Bank, to its affiliated organizations, or to any individual acting in their behalf.

Library of Congress Cataloging in Publication Data

Gupta, Syamaprasad, 1928–
A model for income distribution, employment, and growth.
(World Bank staff occasional paper; no. 24)
Bibliography: p. 120
1. Income distribution—Indonesia—Mathematical models. 2. Indonesia—Economic policy. I. Title. II. Series.
HC450.I5G86 339.2′09598 76–53909
ISBN 0–8018–1950–4

Foreword

I WOULD LIKE TO EXPLAIN why the World Bank does research work and why this research is published. We feel an obligation to look beyond the projects that we help finance toward the whole resource allocation of an economy and the effectiveness of the use of those resources. Our major concern, in dealings with member countries, is that all scarce resources—including capital, skilled labor, enterprise, and know-how—should be used to their best advantage. We want to see policies that encourage appropriate increases in the supply of savings, whether domestic or international. Finally, we are required by our Articles, as well as by inclination, to use objective economic criteria in all our judgments.

These are our preoccupations, and these, one way or another, are the subjects of most of our research work. Clearly, they are also the proper concern of anyone who is interested in promoting development, and so we seek to make our research papers widely available. In doing so, we have to take the risk of being misunderstood. Although these studies are published by the Bank, the views expressed and the methods explored should not necessarily be considered to represent the Bank's views or policies. Rather, they are offered as a modest contribution to the great discussion on how to advance the economic development of the underdeveloped world.

ROBERT S. MCNAMARA
President
The World Bank

Contents

Figures

Preface

Syamaprasad Gupta's modest work on income distribution, growth, and employment in Indonesia is an important one for the World Bank and for the development community. Not only does it break new ground in the treatment of nongrowth development objectives and show that in many instances they are indeed compatible with those of growth, but, more important, it represents the first fruits of an effort, begun more than five years ago, to bridge the ever-increasing gap between modelbuilders and the policymakers for whom such models are supposed to be designed. Gupta's model grew out of Bank operational economic missions to Indonesia and was used to answer a variety of questions in that context long before it evolved to its present form. It is even now being used by the government of Indonesia.

The fact that the Gupta model breaks new ground in the theory and practice of income distribution adds to the value of this work for the development community as a whole. Previously, the theory suggested that income redistribution always had a growth tradeoff. This model opens up a large new area of analysis by demonstrating that the question of a tradeoff between growth and equity depends on the specific policies adopted to redistribute and that in certain cases it is even possible to have redistribution and an *increase* in growth.

This illumination of new issues in income distribution occurred not as the result of academic curiosity but because operational decisionmakers needed fairly immediate answers to these questions.

Over the past fifteen years, many attempts have been made to build models for developing countries, but few have been successful either academically or operationally. A paucity of data and a rapidly changing structure have plagued modelbuilders, and local institutions have not been strong enough to use and maintain the models once they were made. A well-trained economist tends to be interested in illuminating structure. For this he uses data of the past to try to say something about what might occur in the future. In a developing economy, however, data are unreliable and for key variables may never have been collected. Even where the data do exist and are collected and where the model is estimated in timely fashion, conditions and structure may have changed significantly by the time the model is available, rendering it operationally useless.

In contrast, policymakers need to make immediate decisions and often have hunches that have served them well in the past. They thus tend to make small, informal models "on the back of an envelope," using whatever data are on hand and relying heavily on heuristic information. The success record of such models has been high, but they are rarely formalized and would appear to be at continual odds with economic and econometric theory and practice. When modelbuilder and policymaker sit together they usually understand and agree with each other, but when it comes to putting their thoughts into model form, the results are strikingly different. The economist is struck by the policymaker's grasp of, and dependence upon, specific detail and his need to answer very specific questions, but when the modeler tries to bring his craft to this level he finds almost no hard data, and his model takes too long to build and keep up to date.

The Gupta model of Indonesia comes from a tradition that makes a conscious effort to bridge this gap. The philosophy of such a model is that it should be economically sound and econometrically correct; it should focus upon answering the specific questions of the policymaker; it should integrate as much heuristic information from the policymaker as possible; it should be timely; and it should be easily usable by local institutions. The model contained in this book meets these objectives better than any before it and as such represents a significant milestone in the construction of models for developing countries.

Nicholas G. Carter
Chief, Comparative Analysis and Projections Division
The World Bank

Acknowledgments

THIS PAPER IS BASED on a model initially prepared for the World Bank basic economic mission to Indonesia in 1974. In the light of later discussions, it was expanded to explore a few alternative development strategies for the country over the next decade.

I am grateful to Willem Bussink, the chief of the mission, for his intellectual stimulus, advice, and assistance. Also, I have benefited enormously from the help and advice of the other mission members, both from the World Bank and the International Monetary Fund.

I am extremely grateful to Alan Strout, Graham Pyatt, and Jean L. Waelbroeck, and to Wouter Tims, Nicholas G. Carter, and Parvez Hasan for their very valuable comments while the model was being extended. Thanks are also due to Irfan ul Haque, Om Nijhawan, Moh Arsjad Anwar, J. L. Tamba and many other friends and colleagues, both within and outside the Bank, for their advice and editorial assistance. Goddard Winterbottom edited the final manuscript of the book.

SYAMAPRASAD GUPTA

Introduction and Summary

THIS WORK ORIGINATED in connection with a World Bank mission to Indonesia in 1974 to prepare a basic economic report on the country. Its structure is therefore largely influenced by the needs of the mission. An attempt is made to explore the growth potential of the Indonesian economy, as well as the effects on employment and income distribution and other consequences of adopting alternative development strategies. One of the primary goals is to explore the tradeoff between equity and growth in the long-term context of these alternative strategies.

The whole exercise has been confined to a formal quantitative framework and therefore encounters the difficulty of trying to quantify many of the noneconomic aspects of the development process. Standard modeling procedure is improved, however, by introducing a measure of the quality of growth, as opposed to a mere quantification. For example, most existing macroeconomic models display a virtually unqualified commitment to growth (measured as a quantity) as the primary objective of development strategy. This assumption is not because growth is regarded as a legitimate end in itself but because growth has been widely believed to be a necessary and sufficient condition for the elimination of poverty and unemployment. Empirical evidence appears to indicate, however, that although growth is necessary it alone is not sufficient to realize this dual objective.

The purpose of this book is therefore to explore the tradeoffs between growth and equity, growth and employment, and growth and poverty. Growth as used herein is defined as the percentage change in gross domestic product (GDP); equity, as a reduction in the Gini coefficient (a measure of relative income distribution);

and poverty, as a measure of absolute standard of living of the poorest. Quantitatively, poverty is calculated as the total money transfer needed to raise all people above a minimum standard of living, with this total expressed as a percentage of their total income. Thus, an attempt is made to reflect the growing awareness in the World Bank and among the developing countries of the importance of ensuring the quality of life in the pursuit of general economic development. Other studies have addressed this problem, but only through the use of partial equilibrium analysis. The novelty of the Indonesia study is its treatment of the problem from the point of view of a general equilibrium, integrating the results of economic activity on a national basis.

As demonstrated in the following chapters growth can be increased by sacrificing, to a certain extent, a nation's quality of life—that is, by diminishing the standard of living among the poor, or by causing a deterioration of income distribution throughout society. This, clearly, poses an interesting problem for the policy planner: If there is a choice in the development process of a given country between growth for its own sake and the distribution of growth's benefits among the masses, what are the criteria for determining the nature of a policy tradeoff? Further, can a development strategy be chosen that will maximize net social benefits?

Two set of conclusions are drawn from the analysis presented here. The first concerns the pattern of development observed in Indonesia. Among developing countries there is a growing awareness of the importance of underemployment and unemployment, which is reflected in their national policies. Indonesia is no exception. Like the rest of the developing world, it is heading toward a more uneven distribution of income unless the government intervenes with an active distributive policy. Indonesia's growth shows an urban bias, with heavy emphasis on the organized industrial sector. Such a bias sets the stage for a more uneven distribution of income, a lower rate of employment, and a higher pressure on foreign exchange resources. Unlike many other developing countries, however, Indonesia has benefited from the recent rise in oil prices. This benefit has accrued mainly as government revenue, which enhances significantly the role of the public sector investment program in Indonesia.

The second set of conclusions comprises policy lessons drawn from alternative development strategies. First, the question of a tradeoff between equity and growth can be explored only in the context of specific policy measures. Any generalization about growth and income distribution is inadvisable without reference to a specific country or stage of development or without consideration of the whole range of policy strategies. Within the restricted range of feasible policies in Indonesia a choice between the two goals seems unavoidable, but there is room to maneuver for social priorities so that policies will be selected to *optimize* growth and income distribution.

Second, to attack the problem of unemployment an *active* employment policy must be implemented. A strategy that is exclusively growth oriented, without a conscious employment effort, might not be successful in reducing unemployment, because there is only a weak correlation between growth and employment.

Third, to eliminate poverty, that is, to attain a certain minimum standard of living, an employment policy is more effective than a policy directed exclusively toward growth.

Fourth, the relation between growth and income distribution is significantly affected by the set of policy tools available to the public authorities, and the relevant policies are not confined to income distribution alone. For example, the relations between growth and distribution will be directly affected by any specific public action to bring the economy to a state of equilibrium from an initial imbalance of supply and demand.

Finally, with a change in the assumption about the future growth of population, predicted growth and employment are not influenced in the short or medium term, but over a longer period changes in demographic patterns would have a very significant effect. Hence, in formulating any prospective plan for Indonesia, population policy should be given a high priority.

A Model
for Income Distribution, Employment, and Growth

1

Definitions and Assumptions

THE FOLLOWING SECTIONS contain a general discussion of a few common hypotheses regarding the relations between and among growth, equity, and employment. These hypotheses are tested empirically in subsequent chapters of the study.

The Growth-Equity Tradeoff

The tradeoff between growth and equity conventionally is illustrated by an equity-growth curve, with a negative slope, as shown in Figure 1. The y-axis measures equity (that is, 1 minus the Gini coefficient, or $1-G$); the x-axis measures the percentage rate of growth in GDP over the same period. The curve CB measures the rate of substitution of one goal against the other: that is, equity against growth. The preference curve GG' represents the social welfare function. Thus, the optimal combination of growth and equity, which maximizes social welfare, is point A.

But in reality the relation of growth and equity is not as simple. It depends largely on the policy instruments used for attaining any growth rate. The relation also depends on the particular stage or level of development of a society, as well as on the kinds of change taking place. Hence, the relation is dependent on the stage of development in relation to equity; growth and equity, which implies the issue as to whether greater growth means more equitable distribution; and growth with equity, which implies the question as to whether any growth must be sacrificed to achieve positive redistributive policies. A subtle difference between the second and the

Figure 1. The Tradeoff between Equity and Growth

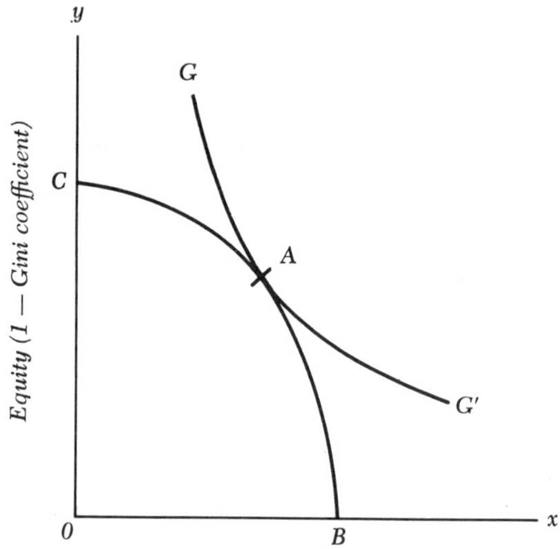

Annual growth rate of GDP

third cases is that in the second case the growth effects are studied against a distribution-neutral policy, whereas in the third case a positive redistributive policy is presumed.

Accordingly the tradeoff hypothesis was reformulated into three parts. First, stage of development and equity has a U-shaped relation.[1] In Figure 2 equity is measured along the y-axis (the value 1 minus the Gini coefficient) and per capita income over time along the x-axis; the $BB'C$ curve represents the functional relation between the two. As a country's per capita income improves, the income distribution is in general seen to deteriorate until it reaches a minimum level. Beyond that point, B', income distribution improves with every increase in per capita income. Thus, BB' shows the relevant relation expected in the early stage of a country's economic development. Its causation is both complex and country specific. One principal explanation could be, however, that there exists a

1. This has been borrowed from Kuznets' hypothesis tested against cross-sectional data. See Simon Kuznets, "Economic Growth and Income Inequality," *American Economic Review*, vol. 45, no. 1 (1955), pp. 1–28.

Figure 2. The Functional Relation between Equity and per Capita Income

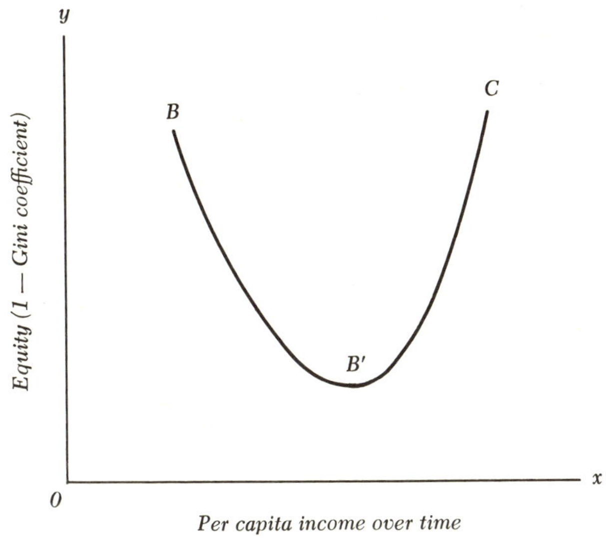

high level of underemployment and unemployment, a low bargaining power of labor, and the use of production techniques that permit an unskilled and low-paid labor force.

Second, growth and equity have a positive correlation in a distribution-neutral policy complex. If, as in Figure 3, a country is at initial position *A* and embarks on a distribution-neutral growth policy, it can grow along alternative growth paths from high to low, as in AP_4 or AP_3 or AP_2 . . . AP_1. According to this hypothesis, all the slopes are upward bending and therefore show no tradeoff between growth and equity. Again, a host of factors can explain this, but it would seem most likely that employment generation among the low-income class might best explain this phenomenon.

Growth has a negative relation with equity in a redistributive policy complex. This relation is better understood when viewed from the opposite end: that is, income distribution affecting growth (see Figure 4). If a country, starting from initial position *A*, adopts positive redistributive policies, growth in every case will decline. A causal relation would presume that the forces hindering growth,

Figure 3. Alternative Paths of Growth under Distributive-Neutral Growth Policies

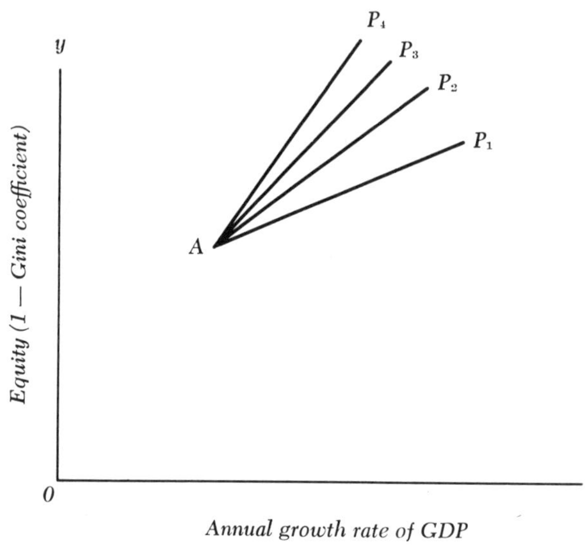

the result of redistributive measures, will outweigh the forces encouraging growth.

The simulation exercises discussed later reveal, however, that the above relation is not as simple and direct. Conceptually, when income equality increases, two opposing sets of forces start working, one set hindering growth, the other encouraging it. The principal forces hindering growth include the following:

—Aggregate saving will decline because poor people have a lower propensity to save.
—The volume of exports will decline because domestic consumption is likely to compete with exports.
—Investment could decline because incentives of the entrepreneurs might be adversely affected.[2]

The principal forces encouraging growth include the following:

2. This, of course, would depend largely on policy instruments used to bring the changes in income inequality.

Figure 4. The Negative Relation between Equity and Growth under Redistributive Policies

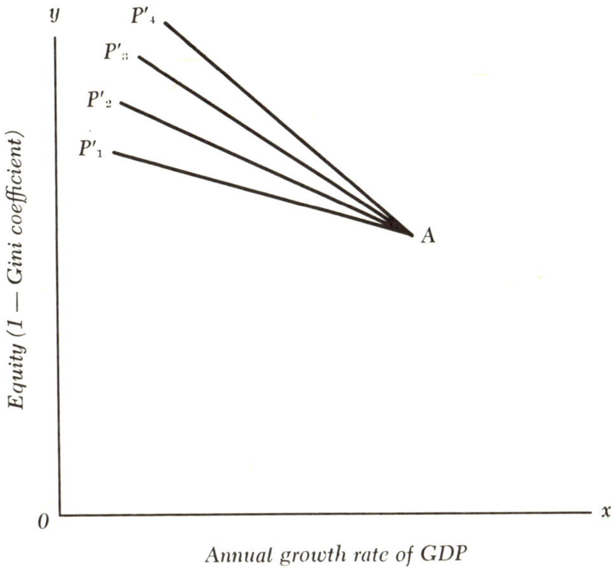

—The income shift to the poorer classes will change the demand pattern in favor of goods produced by the labor-intensive sectors. This would improve the growth potential in labor-abundant capital-scarce economies. A part of this favorable effect might, however, be canceled out by a shift of demand from services to commodity sectors, that is, from low to high import areas.

—The income shift to the poorer classes will reduce the volume of imports, on the assumption that the propensity of the poor people to import is less than the average. This would relax the foreign exchange constraints and facilitate growth.

—Assuming that poor people have a higher propensity to consume, the demand-oriented sectors would grow faster.

—The improvements in the standard of living for the very poor—those below the minimum standard—might increase the productivity of both labor and capital and thereby encourage growth.

The Growth-Employment Tradeoff

The relation between growth and employment has generally been assumed to be of a direct nature. For example, it is assumed that any increase in growth will increase employment. The one way to guarantee the direct relation is to assume that the economy will grow, without a change in its sectoral composition, and the changes in labor-capital substitution will operate only in relation to incremental output.

As shown in Figure 5, OE^*E' is the employment-output curve; when output increases, employment increases. Growth is constrained either by full employment (EE') or by supply of other inputs ($GrGr'$). Hence, there is no tradeoff between growth and employment.

In reality, however, the relation is not that straightforward. If

Figure 5. The Direct Relation between Growth and Employment

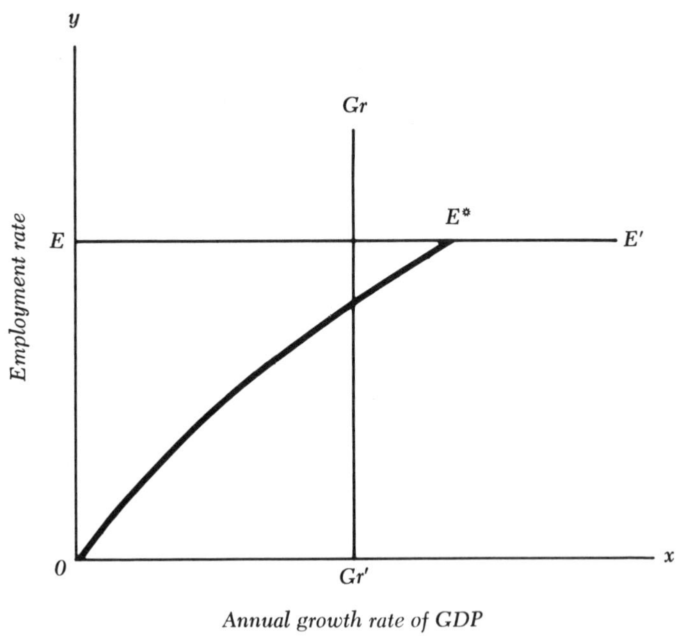

the sector composition of GDP is allowed to change or if a change in production technique is permitted, the tradeoff between employment and growth would appear conspicuously. Referring to Figure 6, OI_1, OI_2, OI_3 . . . and so on give the alternative growth-employment curves for different GDP sector mix and techniques of production. When rates of growth increase from OD to OD_1, employment might increase from Da_1 to $D_1a'_1$, $D_1a'_2$, or$D_1a'_3$, or might decrease to $D_1a'_4$, depending on the choice of different paths for development and technology. Thus, any generalization about the relation between growth and employment is not possible.

The Growth-Poverty Tradeoff

As has been discussed in earlier paragraphs, growth in many cases is directly related to employment, which is believed to be directly

Figure 6. Alternative Patterns of Growth and Employment with Changes in Sector Mix and Production Techniques

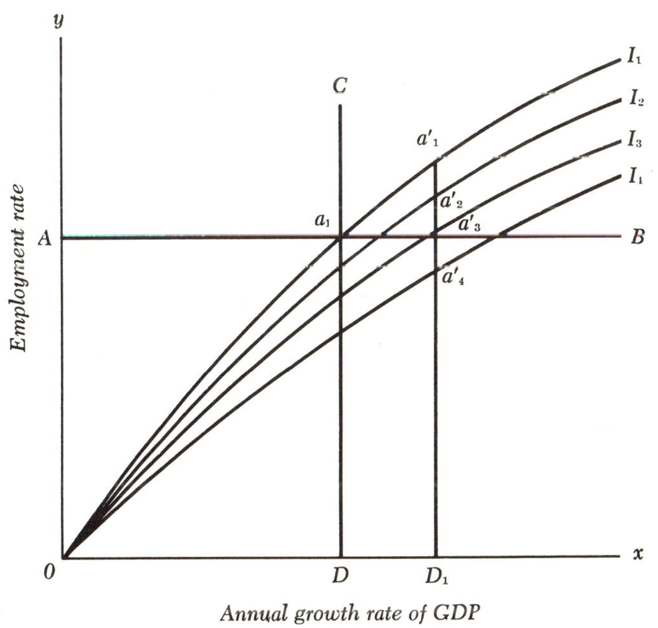

related to the reduction in poverty. Higher growth will employ more people, and the unemployed labor force living below the poverty line will be smaller. But a reduction in poverty might not lead to a general reduction in the income disparity of all classes (as measured by the Gini coefficient), at least not in a conspicuous sense. The empirical findings of the case tend to support this view.

Special Features of the Model

There are several excellent studies linking income distribution and growth.[3] Most of them, however, have open ends. Some try to trace the effects of alternative income distribution patterns on employment and outputs; others try to measure the impact of given growth strategies on income distribution. In this study an attempt is made to close this loop: to show, that is, an income distribution affecting growth and a growth affecting income distribution. Diagrammatically, as shown in Figure 7, it is as follows: *I* is the investment vector (*l* is gestation lag); *Y* is the output vector; *In* is the income vector; *E* is the expenditure vector; *WF* is the working force; *Pf* represents production functions; *CL* is the capital-labor market; *SAV* is savings; *PUBF* is public finance; *e* is consumption elasticity; and *t* refers to a time concept.

In a very simplified causal relation, past investment determines output via the production functions. Output determines income (and distribution) via the factor market and asset distribution. Income generates consumption demand and savings. Consumption demand influences future demand for capacity generation. Saving supplies the investable surplus.[4] In most other studies the link is developed from *In* to *Y*, but the loop remains open. But in a closed-loop model, output will generate income, income will generate saving and expenditure, and saving and expenditure will generate output—in a dynamic sequence.

Furthermore, the principal concern of this study has been a more comprehensive one: to make alternative projections of major economic variables in the Indonesian economy, given different policy

3. See especially F. Paukert, "Redistribution of Income, Patterns of Consumption and Employment: A Case Study for the Philippines," International Labour Organisation Working Paper, 1974.

4. For a more detailed flow chart, see Figure 8.

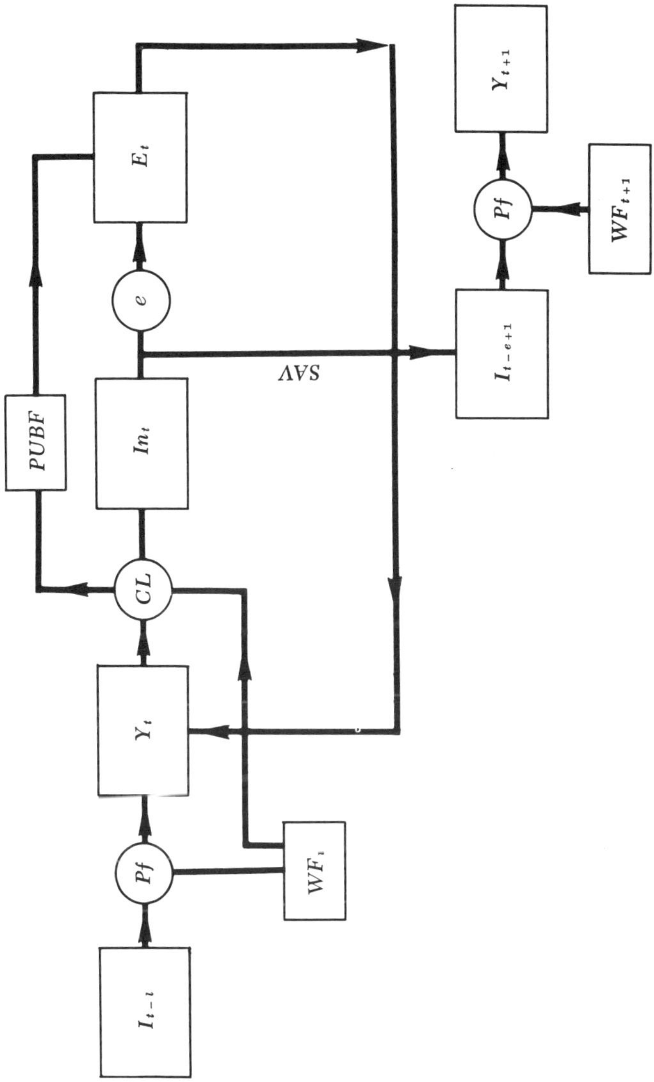

Figure 7. The Relations among Income Distribution, Employment, and GDP

alternatives, aid availabilities, and technological possibilities. Therefore, the sensitivity analysis is confined to a restricted feasibility set only. The testing of an alternative hypothesis regarding relations among income distribution, growth, and employment is limited to this feasibility range.

For this purpose a model has been developed with the following special features:

—The national income balance is secured at current price.
—The price vector is endogenous.
—The saving-investment gap and the export-import gap are equated by means of changes in relative prices and allocation of resources.
—Income distribution is directly related to the production process and the labor market.
—Monetary, fiscal, and real variables are interrelated.
—Saving and consumption are estimated directly and not as residuals, as in most national income models.
—Material balances are secured for all principal sectors: rice, other agriculture, tree crops, fishing, meat, vegetables, capital food, intermediate goods,[5] consumption goods (manufactured), services, trade, banking, transport, mining, and construction.

The choice of specification of the present model has been constrained by three principal considerations: the purpose of the investigation; the existing structure and strategy of development; and the availability of data.

The first point has been discussed earlier. As to the second consideration, the existing structure of the Indonesian economy has been shaped largely by two historical circumstances: a prolonged period of colonial rule and a decade of political instability during the late 1950s and early 1960s. Among the consequences of these was the development of a dualistic economy with a dominant foreign-owned sector comprising plantation and mining and a primitive domestic-activity sector comprising agriculture and rural industry. The first sector can be described as an enclave economy having no multiplier impact on the rest of the society. Its employment component was negligible and most of its investment was in imported capital goods. The only links between sector and the rest of the economy were in contributions to the revenue of the government and to the export earnings of the non-oil economy (net of its own imports). This contribution was relatively insignificant, however, before the oil boom began in 1974; the contribution from oil revenue to govern-

5. Intermediate goods demand equals domestic output of intermediate goods plus imports plus an input-substitution factor (with a maximum ceiling) as technical progress.

ment revenue was as low as 15 percent in 1971-72, compared with more than 50 percent in 1975.

A complete depletion of the existing capital stock occurred during the decade of political instability between 1959-68, when no significant investment was made even to replace the existing capital consumption. The percentage decrease of investment was 30 percent between 1961 and 1967, whereas it increased by 254 percent between 1967 and 1973. The former period was one of political and economic uncertainty and stagnation—the economy grew at 1.3 percent a year between 1961 and 1967, as against 6.1 percent a year between 1967 and 1973—flight of capital, high inflation (18,958 percent in 1967, with 1961 equal to 100), high import propensity, heavy government expenditure, and no technological progress.

The population growth was high, 2.1 percent a year; since 1974 it has been forecast to increase further, to 2.4 or 2.5 percent a year, which would result in more unemployment and underemployment.

Recently this gloomy trend has been stemmed by the establishment of a stable government and a discipline in government budgeting and monetary management and the initiation of a program for development. In addition, a substantial increase has occurred in public saving (as revenue from the oil sector) and—especially because of a favorable movement in the world oil prices and prices of a few primary goods—in private saving in specific organized sectors. These latest developments have contributed to a high level of investment activity.

Most of these new investments are concentrated in prestigious, highly capital-intensive sectors with low employment components. This has aggravated unemployment, poverty, and income inequality. Furthermore, in the government's momentum to control past hyperinflation, various credit restriction, far exceeding the need to control current prices, have brought about in a few sectors an absolute decline in real output.

To sum up, growth, employment, income distribution, allocation of sectoral and regional investment, and import substitution as against export promotion are areas in which critical choices must be made in any future development strategy for Indonesia. Any development model for that country must accommodate a proper treatment of all these issues simultaneously.

Availability of data has been the third major consideration in determining specification of the model for Indonesia. Data are too scanty to explore in a more detailed perspective all the relevant issues described above. For example, time series information is almost nonexistent on a comparable footing before 1968. Hence, alternative sources from cross-section and cross-country data have been tapped.

Limitations of the Model

Some of the principal limitations in the specification of this model must be mentioned.

First, this model treats price as a cost-of-production markup. Over a long and medium time horizon this assumption seems to be quite realistic. Furthermore, if the main purpose of this exercise is to present the likely equilibrium picture of the economy in the future—subject to certain changes in the policies and exogenous variables and free from uncertainties—the price should approximate cost.

Second, the present model should not be identified as a pure general equilibrium model, because neither investment nor consumption in the model are price elastic. There is also no functional relation between asset formation and return on capital.

Third, the model assumes that real wages change in response to changes in cost of living and level of unemployment. It has not attempted to allocate positively any share of labor productivity (expressed as output per worker), since it is assumed that at a low level of employment and with an unorganized labor market there exists no systematic productivity-sharing scheme that works through employer-employee dialogue. This assumption, again, seems to be realistic in the Indonesian context.

Fourth, the assumption that the lowest two income classes are all wage earners may not be realistic. This assumption has been necessary because of lack of information regarding self-employed persons, but it may not create significant bias in the result.

2

Mechanics of the Model

IN THIS MODEL the growth of sectoral output is governed by considerations of either demand or supply. There are, however, a few sectors in which factors of both the supply and the demand influence output and at any point of time only one set of factors becomes binding. Personal services, for example, grow in response to pressures of demand until full employment is reached, after which the growth is governed by the available labor force. In medium- and large-scale industries, also, growth is at first constrained by the availability of investable funds, but beyond a certain point the binding constraint becomes the supply of skilled labor.

Over a longer period of time and at a higher stage of development, when a near-full employment is reached, a country can accelerate its growth only by diverting its investable resources toward more capital-intensive techniques. This requires, however, an increased supply of skilled labor and therefore more investment in education, training, and research.

Besides the constraints of labor, capital, and demand, another binding constraint is important in a country's growth process: the trade constraint, which arises out of a shortage of foreign exchange earnings. If a country suffers from a scarcity of foreign exchange, it can adopt one or all of the following measures:

—It can substitute for imports by developing alternative domestic sources, by developing new production techniques and economizing on certain inputs, or by changing the output mix and enlarging sectors with a lower import component.

—It can change exchange rates and encourage use of domestic inputs.
—It can reduce growth and make suboptimal use of domestic saving potentialities.

The present model has explored each of these measures to cope with the trade constraint. Each of the measures has a different impact on growth, employment, income distribution, and economic efficiency.

Alternative strategies of export promotion and import substitution have also been explored in relation to growth, employment, and income distribution.

In the simulation exercises, several runs have been extended beyond 1985 to explore certain long-term issues. Of course, some confidence in the estimated parameters used has thereby been sacrificed.

The model consists of a set of nonlinear equations and simulates activities from year to year.[1] Each year's solution is dependent on current and preceding values of variables, but not on future ones. An attempt has been made to incorporate the future by forming expectations from past changes and future values of certain exogenous variables that can be regarded as targets in many instances.

The present model has two sets of specifications: to satisfy a need for operational use, as in the writing of economic reports in the World Bank; and to explore the entire relation between and among growth, income distribution, and employment in a comparatively disaggregated general equilibrium frame.

This study focuses on the second specification in more detail. In the first specification, the number of exogenous variables were very large and based primarily on the assessment by sectoral experts in the light of their feasibility. This first approach gave the model a strong projection, or forecasting, bias—but its specification is rather poor for policy purposes. Many of the exogenous variables used were conceptually related to one another. For example, the growth of agricultural output, investment, and fertilizer were all exogenous in the model, although in reality they should have been functionally related to one another. This approach makes impossible any sensitivity analysis of each of the factors.

In the second specification of the model a large number of these

1. There are approximately 700 equations, solved recursively for each year.

exogenous variables are made endogenous; only variables that are genuinely independent of one another are kept exogenous. The functional relations between these variables are estimated in two stages. Initially, they were estimated from time series or cross-section analysis from country data. In the second stage they were revised in the light of explicit or implicit parameters used by sectoral experts or in official economic documents. In the first specification of the model an attempt was made to adhere to an economic classification close to the official one in order to facilitate a dialogue with the Indonesian government. But in the second specification there was further disaggregation—sometimes in the light of special surveys—in order to develop relevant economic relations.

The model has the following blocks of relations:

Production	Fiscal policy
Consumption	Prices
Investment	Monetary policy
Income distribution and employment	Exports and imports
	Capital transactions
Savings	Population

The Production Block

Output growth in a sector is constrained by either lack of demand or lack of supply. Further, output in a few key sectors, including the public sector, is guided by public policy. The production function of each sector has been treated in decomposed form; marginal capital coefficients and labor elasticities (in response to output) are assumed to be constant or changing exogenously. When the labor elasticity is less than 1, it presumes a substitution of capital for labor or technical progress. There are altogether twenty-three activity sectors, of which five are exogenous (E), eight are supply constrained (S), and ten are demand oriented (D). The sectors are the following:

Rice (S)	Fishing (D)
Tree crops (S)	Vegetables (D)[2]
Other agriculture (S)	Livestock (D)[3]
Forestry (E)	Mineral (E)

2. For production in low land, supply constraint is more effective.
3. Some supply constraint operates through imported feed grains.

Capital goods industry (S)
Intermediate goods industry (S)
Consumption goods industry (labor-intensive) (S)
Consumption of goods industry (capital-intensive) (S)
Small-scale traditional industries (D)
Construction (D)
Dwellings (E)
Trade (D)
Transport (D)
Banking and professional services (D)
Public administration (E)
Electricity (D)
Services (D)
Public works (E)
Labor-absorbing sectors (comprising agriculture, trade, and services) (S)

The sectors constrained by supply are classified into two groups:

—Growth is constrained by the supply of material inputs such as land, fertilizer, and irrigational facilities. The supply of these inputs is exogenously determined. Rice, tree crops, and other agriculture fall into this group.
—Growth is constrained by the supply of investable funds. The investable funds are constrained by availability of domestic and foreign saving after the demand for investment in the demand-oriented sectors are met. The large-scale manufacturing sectors belong to this group.

The sectors constrained by demand are also classified in two groups:

—Growth is constrained principally by demand from final consumers.
—Growth is constrained principally by demand from intermediate users.

The first is estimated by expenditure elasticities of different income classes (households). Fishing, vegetables, and livestock fall in this group. The second is estimated either by the intermediate input requirements of the producing sectors (construction and electricity), or by broad demand elasticities derived from national income accounts for those sectors in which their detailed contribution to all other sectors are not available (trade, transport, banking services, and small-scale industry), or by both.

The exogenous sectors are classified in two groups:

—The first is decided by the public authorities.
—The second is decided by forces outside the control of the country.

Further, three sectors—agriculture, services, and trade—are assumed to absorb the unemployed labor force at a very low marginal productivity (which, of course, reduces the average income in these sectors). Hence, the overall growth rates of these sectors are affected to some extent by the working population and the level of activity in the rest of the economy.

Two major sectors are affected by labor constraint (after full employment is reached): the personal services sector, which grows according to the available labor supply after the demand from all other sectors is met; and the organized industry sector, in which the upper limit to growth is set by the supply of skilled manpower. In the present model the rate of expansion of skilled manpower is stipulated exogenously.

The following paragraphs outline in greater detail how the value added in the different sectors is computed.

Agriculture. The agriculture sector consists of five subsectors.

For rice, the total output is the sum of rice grown on irrigated land and that grown on nonirrigated land. The ouput from irrigated is a function of the land and fertilizer available. The growth rates for land and fertilizer are exogenously determined. In the basic simulation they are 2.4 percent a year for land and 10 percent a year for fertilizer and as inputs. The rice output from nonirrigated land depends solely upon land available; it has an exogenously determined growth rate of 3 percent.

For tree crops, the output is a function of the land areas, the 3.5 percent growth rate of which is exogenous.

For other agriculture, output is determined in a manner similar to tree crops, with an additional time trend added.

For forestry, output is determined by an exogenous growth rate of 10 percent.

For vegetables, fish, and livestock, the output is determined by domestic and export demand for these commodities. Their annual growth rate is limited to a maximum of 8 percent.

Large-scale manufacturing. The large-scale manufacturing sector comprises the production of capital goods, intermediate goods, and consumption goods (labor and capital intensive). The growth in output in each case is determined by the investment and an exogenous, constant (over time) marginal capital productivity. Investments in these industries have a three-year gestation lag except for labor-intensive consumption goods, for which the lag is two years.

The annual growth rate in these industries is limited to 30 percent except for capital goods, for which the growth rate cannot exceed 50 percent. These limits on the growth rate are the result of the rate at which skilled labor can be increased in the economy. The example below shows how the value added in the capital goods industry is calculated for 1985:

$$VA\ Cap_t = VA\ Cap_{t-1} + \frac{1}{3} \times \left(\sum_{i=1}^{-3} Inv_i \right) \times \text{ICOR}^{-1},$$

where *VA Cap* is defined as value added in the capital goods industry in period *t*, Inv_i as investment in period *i*, and ICOR as incremental capital-output ratio.

Traditional manufacturing. The output is determined by the increase in demand, which in turn is a function of the disposable income of the population.

Minerals. The output of the mineral industry, excluding oil, is determined by an 8 percent exogenous growth rate.

Construction. The construction industry's output is calculated as the construction component of investment in the economy. The construction component of investment in minerals, mining, and transportation is 30 percent, whereas that of other investments is 45 percent.

Trade, transportation, and banking. The output of these sectors is governed by the demand from the manufacturing sector. For every 1 percent increase in the value added of manufactured goods, the value added in each of these sectors rises by 1.1 percent.

Services. The output of this sector is determined on the same basis as the three sectors above except that the percentage increase in value added is directly proportional to the increase in value-added goods.

Dwellings. The value added in dwellings—that is, rental income—is determined by an exogenously determined growth rate of 5 percent.

Electricity. Electricity generation is determined by the sum of industrial and consumer demand. Industrial demand is determined by the production of capital, intermediate, and consumption goods. Direct consumer demand is assumed to be 0.14 percent of GDP. For example, in 1985 the value added was determined as follows in the basic solution:

$$VA\ Elect = (VA\ Cap \times 0.45 + VA\ Int \times 0.196 + VA\ Con(Trad) \times 0.035 + VA\ Con(Mod) \times 0.085 + 0.0014 \times \text{GDP}) \times 0.7,$$

where *VA Elect* is defined as value added in electricity and *VA Cap*, *VA Int*, *VA Con(Trad)*, *VA Con(Mod)*, and GDP as, respectively, value added in the capital goods industry, the intermediate goods industry, the consumption goods industry of the traditional type, the consumption goods industry of the modern type, and final consumers' demand (for which gross domestic product serves as proxy).

Public works. The output of this sector is determined autonomously by the public authorities as public works programs in the rural sector.

Public administration. The value added is a function of the outputs of goods, transportation, and banking.

Labor absorption. The model does not allow any open unemployment. The unemployment is disguised by having the excess labor absorbed at a very low productivity in the agriculture, services, and trade sectors.

Oil output has been treated separately in the model. The GDP has been divided into two parts, oil and non-oil. The oil sector's only contribution to the non-oil sector is in the form of oil revenues to the government and foreign exchange earnings to the export sector, net of oil sector's imports.[4]

The Consumption Block

Consumption is divided into private and public consumption. Public consumption is exogenous and is assumed to remain at a constant percentage of GDP at factor cost. Private consumption per capita is calculated by subtracting the per capita savings from per capita current disposable household income. Total consumption is estimated by multiplying per capita consumption by the number of persons in the respective income classes.

The Investment Block

Total investable funds are determined as the sum of total domestic savings and net transfers from abroad. These funds are first invested

4. $VA_{(n.o.)} + Rev_{(o)} = (C + I)_{n.o.} + E_{n.o.} + (E - M)_o - M_{n.o.}$,
$VA_{(o)} = (C + I)_o + E_o - M_o$, and
$(C + I)_o = M_o$,
where $n.o.$ = non-oil, o = oil, VA = value added, Rev = revenue, C = consumption, E = Export, M = Import, and I = Investment.

where investment is exogenously determined, as in mining, capital replacement (1 percent of GDP), and increase in working capital (20 percent of change in GDP). Investment is then made in the demand-oriented sectors. The required investment in these sectors is determined on the basis of change in output, marginal investment-output ratios, and gestation periods. Appendix B shows the ratios and gestation lags for different sectors. The residual investable funds are then allocated to the capital, intermediate, and consumption goods industries.[5] The initial allocation is as follows: capital goods, 7.7 percent; intermediate goods, 55.2 percent; consumption (labor intensive), 12.6 percent; and consumption (capital intensive), 24.5 percent. It is assumed, however, that Indonesia cannot compete in world export markets for manufactured consumption goods, so if production exceeds domestic demand the above allocation ratios are changed to keep production and demand in balance. These ratios are 24.8 percent, 55.2 percent, 5 percent, and 15 percent, respectively.

The Income Distribution and Employment Block

Conceptually, it is possible to simulate the pattern of income distribution over time, as a continuous function of policy variables, through their effects on production, factor and asset incomes,[6] and the pattern of consumption as a function of a given income distribution; this would have closed the loop of the distribution block. Empirically, however, it has not been possible to relate the specific policy variables to individual parameters, describing the income distribution in a continuous sense. Therefore, a simpler approach has been adopted. For the base period, ten activity sectors and four income classes were specified. The activity sectors are agriculture, large- and medium-scale industry, small-scale industry, construction, electricity, transport, banking and professional services, public administration, services, and trade.

5. If the investment decisions in those sectors were made under competitive market conditions, the allocation of investments would be according to values of marginal products. But in Indonesia the investment decisions in the organized industry are guided mostly by considerations of national policy by the public authorities (or Investment Board). Hence, they were assumed to be exogenous in the model.

6. This depends on the cumulative net saving of each income group and the rate of return on savings invested in assets.

The four income classes correspond to monthly per capita incomes of Rp 0–1,000, Rp 1,000–2,000, Rp 2,000–4,000, and Rp 4,000 and above, at 1969 prices (to match the 1969 family expenditure study).[7] The mean income of each income group will, of course, change over the simulation period. The income size (class) distribution will change over time in response to the following conditions: (a) different growth rates between labor income (determined by the labor market) and returns on capital or assets (determined by the asset market); (b) different output growth rates of the ten activity sectors; (c) changing composition of factor inputs (labor and capital), depending on the nature of the production functions (that is, technological changes and factor substitution); (d) changes in the structure of marginal asset ownership (depending on the cumulative net saving of each income group and the rate of return on savings invested in assets); (e) changes in internal and external terms of trade; (f) changes in the pattern of tax subsidy; and (g) changes in institutional structure. In the present model, the changes in technology, labor-capital substitution, fiscal and monetary policies, and international price movement have been made exogenous.

Besides the Gini coefficient, a poverty coefficient has also been computed as the following ratio: the total money transfer needed to bring everybody up to a minimum poverty level divided by the total earnings of all at this minimum level. The poverty line has been estimated on the basis of the cost of the minimum nutrition needed to survive.

For each of the ten activity sectors, the composition of the labor force between the four income classes has been kept unchanged over the simulation period. An implicit assumption in this context is that the skill mix (of labor use) and the size of the production units (employer to employee) will not be changing over the simulation period. It has been assumed, further, that a skill category of labor is related to its relative ranking in earnings.

The average productivity change for each labor category is the same as the average sectoral productivity change, which is derived from sectoral output changes and employment elasticities.

The average income of each labor category will change depending on the changes in the unit factor income of that class. The rate of

7. Republic of Indonesia, *Survey Sosial Ekonomi Nasional* (National socio-economic survey), October–December 1969 (Jakarta: Central Bureau of Statistics, 1972).

change in the nominal factor income is dependent on the changes in cost of living, with a time lag, and on the level of unemployment, reflecting the scarcity in the labor market.

Another source of income for laborers may accrue from ownership of new assets. This incremental nonwage income will originate from the gains of new ownership of assets. In the model these gains have been treated as income from accumulated savings (cumulated from the base). The ruling market rate of interest is used as the rate of return from capital assets.

The average income of the highest income class (assuming this class will constitute predominantly of entrepreneurs) is treated as a residual, after the lower classes are paid their labor and nonwage incomes.

Savings in each class are estimated separately for each income class and related to their disposable income (that is, net of tax-subsidy).

Since the model hypothesized that open unemployment does not exist, the problem of unemployment is treated in a different way, involving two stages. First, total unemployment has been estimated for the whole economy on the basis of production functions (employment elasticities)[8] and age distribution of the population. Second, unemployed labor is absorbed by the agriculture, trade, and services sector, which have a very low average productivity.

Accordingly, when the unemployed labor is absorbed, the average income of the lowest income class of that sector will be reduced. This appears to indicate that the lower the rate of unemployment, the less the extent of poverty (defined as the average income of the lowest income class below a minimum nutritional level) and the greater the likelihood of improvement in income distribution.

The dependency ratios of each income class and for each sector are estimated from a demographic submodel.[9] From this information the average income and the population for each class and sector are then estimated.

Finally, average income and population distribution are estimated on the basis of a sectoral income distribution. For the sake of simplicity, the model uses the same four income classes as in the

8. In addition, 2 percent of the labor force is assumed to be employed in the mining industry, and the labor force employed in public works is computed by using the value added and assuming that per capita income is Rp 40,000 a year.

9. Dependency ratio is defined as the ratio between population at working age, adjusted by assumed participation rate and total population.

sectoral analysis. This, of course, assumes no overlapping between sectors, though average income in each income class will change over time.

The present approach can be compared with the ICOR approach in investment planning.[10] The initial asset distribution is not known, but the existing income distribution between different classes is known. The incremental changes in this income distribution are affected by the incremental changes in the supply of labor, the changes in unit factor income, and the supply of investable funds (that is, accumulated savings) made by different income class.

The following equations illustrate how the population and average income are calculated for each of the ten sectors:

Labor productivity = labor productivity of the previous year × [1+ (1−employment elasticity) × rate of change of value added].

Income per capita = (labor productivity/dependency ratio) × (sectoral price index/GDP deflator).

Population in a given sector of production = value added × (sectoral price index/GDP deflator)/income per capita.

Population of income class i = population of income class i in the previous year × (population of a given sector of production/total population).

Average income of class 1 = average income of class 1 in the previous year × real wage index + $\left(\sum_{t=1}^{4} \text{real average saving}\right)$ × real rate of return.

Average income of class 2 = average income of class 2 in the previous year × real wage index + $\left(\sum_{t=1}^{4} \text{real average saving}\right)$ × real rate of return.

Average income of class 3 = average income of class 3 in the previous year × (productivity/productivity in the previous year) + $\left(\sum_{t=1}^{4} \text{real average saving}\right)$ × real rate of return.

Average income of class 4 = value added × (sectoral price index/

10. In the ICOR, or incremental capital-output ratio, approach in investment planning, an attempt is made to relate an increase in the level of capital stock with an increase in output. This means that it is not necessary to know the initial capital stock and its distribution.

GDP deflator) $- \left(\sum_{t=1}^{3}\right.$ population of class $i \times$ average income of class $\left. i \right)$/population of class 4 in a given sector.

The wage rate is assumed to be a function of the disguised unemployment rate and the cost of living index. When the unemployment rate is 5 percent, the wage rate keeps pace with the cost of living index. At higher unemployment rates, the increase in the wage rate is slower than the cost of living index, and vice versa at lower rates of unemployment.

Even the estimation of the existing income distribution is not straightforward. This has been attempted on the basis of regional data. The income inequality in any sector is the sum of (a) differences between regions, (b) differences within regions, and (c) overlap of incomes of different regions.[11] In estimating the inequality coefficient, (c) was ignored; the estimates therefore have a statistical bias. For policy purposes, in order to assess the effect on income distribution of alternative fiscal and income policies, only the changes in inequality from year to year were used. Assuming this bias is consistent, the Gini index could be indicative. But, alternatively, if income distribution in countries with large income shifts were neglected and models were computed on the basis of macro savings functions, the results of the model would be likely to be extremely unrealistic.

The Savings Block

Savings are divided into domestic and foreign.

Domestic savings are divided into household, corporate, and government savings. Household saving is derived as a function of disposable income: That is, income net of taxes and subsidies. The propensity to save depends on the average per capita income. Government saving is the difference between government current revenue (including oil revenue) and government expenditure. Corporate saving is equivalent to the depreciation rate in the corporate sector.

11. Graham Pyatt, "On the Interpretation and Disaggregation of Gini Coefficient," *Economic Journal*, vol. 86 (1976), pp. 243–55.

Foreign saving is measured by the current account balance. It is determined on the basis of private and public capital inflow, net of debt service and changes in the foreign exchange reserves.

The Fiscal Block

The fiscal sector consists of government tax and nontax revenues and government current expenditures (including subsidies). Taxes are divided into oil tax, non-oil income tax and corporate tax, taxes on consumption, import tax, and export tax. The tax parameters are derived econometrically at current prices. Government subsidies and current expenditures are exogenous in the models, as are government investments.

The Price Block

Sectoral prices have been estimated by a two-tier approach. In the first tier prices are calculated by adding total direct and indirect labor costs, capital costs, imports costs, and indirect tax payments on intermediate inputs. This was done by Leontief inverse matrix. The interdependence among prices, input structures, and costs of exogenous inputs (value added) is summarized in the familiar input-output accounting identity: $p - pA = v$ or $p = v\ (I - A)^{-1}$ and $p = vQ$, where p is the (row) vector of output prices in each sector, A is the matrix of input-output coefficients, Q is the Leontief inverse, v is the (row) vector of value added per unit of output in each sector, and I is the identity matrix.

The value-added vector consists of labor and capital coefficients per unit of output. They are affected over time by changes in wage rates, rate of return on capital, labor-capital substitution, indirect taxes, import prices, and import component of output.

Changes in sectoral prices result from changes in both total labor requirements and in the skill mix or the wage differentials among sectors. Similarly, changes in the returns on capital, as well as the total capital coefficients in any sector, affect the price system as a whole. Finally, any changes in the import prices (c.i.f.)—that is, changes in exchange rates or world prices—and in the import components of output affect the domestic price structure as well.

In the familiar Leontief price model, capital coefficients, labor coefficients, and labor and capital returns are exogenous. But in this simulation exercise changes in these factors have been integrated in light of the production functions and the factor market conditions chosen in the model. This was done in a loose fashion. The labor coefficients have been made to change on the basis of assumptions of employment elasticities with respect to output. The capital coefficients have been made to change on the basis of marginal and average capital-output ratios.

Labor incomes have been made to change on the assumption that in a high unemployment phase—that is, when the disguised unemployment is high—the rates of labor earnings will catch up with the changes in the cost of living only with a time lag. This means that labor earnings will catch up with the changes in the cost of living with a longer time lag when unemployment is higher. When unemployment falls below a critical point, however, rates of labor earnings begin to increase faster than the changes in the cost of living. At this stage, real wages—real income from labor—will begin to improve.

The import coefficients have been estimated econometrically and have thereafter been changed on the basis of specific information regarding import substitution.

The returns from capital have been divided into normal returns (interest rate, normal profit rate) and abnormal profits. The normal rate of return, which has been made exogenous, is initially set at the level of the international inflation rate. Abnormal profits are the differences between cost and demand price. Estimation of demand price will be discussed in subsequent paragraphs.

The price, thus determined, will include any changes in the production costs of the different sectors. To arrive at the GDP deflator, a combined price index is computed from these sectoral prices. For this purpose the following relation has been used to convert prices originating from gross output (PX) to the prices of industry final demand (PF): PF equals $(I-A)^{-1} D^{-1}PX$,[12] A equals a fixed input-output coefficient matrix, and D^{-1} equals the inverse of a diagonal matrix of the ratio of real gross output to real gross product for each industry.

The cost of living index has been computed from the GDP deflator by computing a composite index, in which the GDP deflator and the

12. B. G. Hickman, ed., *Econometric Models of Cyclical Behavior*, Proceedings of the National Bureau of Economic Research (New York: Columbia University Press, 1972), vol. 1, p. 211.

prices of the imported consumption goods were combined by a given set of weights. The weights used were the consumer expenditure on domestic and foreign goods of the previous year.

Price is also affected by an imbalance of demand and supply. If demand is greater than supply (at a given price), the price will rise—and vice versa. The gap between aggregate demand and supply has been measured by the difference between the demand for, and supply of, money (narrow money). It is assumed further that the inflationary pressure is equally spread in all sectors of the economy.

The new equilibrium is reached when the demand for, and supply of, money equalizes at a higher price. Its effects on real variables will depend on the price sensitivity of consumption and investments. In this analysis it has been assumed that the money supply will always increase as money demand increases. Because of this assumption, there is no "demand-pull inflation" in the calculations.

The Monetary Block

In the monetary sector the attempt is only to formulate a money demand function. There is projected only an optimal rate of increase in the money supply consistent with a certain growth rate, changes in production cost, and changes in people's price expectation for the future. The optimal level of reserve money has also been estimated by using past relations. The private sector balance of payments plus the net claim of the central bank on the nongovernment sector, net of foreign expenditure of the government, have been estimated as residual by subtracting government savings.

The Exports and Imports Block

Conceptually, most of the exports and imports are determined either exogenously or as the difference between domestic production and demand. Export and import prices are mainly exogenous inputs to the model. Exchange rates or tariffs are used to bring exports and imports into balance. This adjustment process is assumed to occur in the markets for intermediate goods.

As to exports, oil, manufacturing, and fish and animal exports are determined exogenously. Exports of tree crops, forestry, and minerals are calculated as the difference between domestic production and demand. These exports, coupled with the net inflow of foreign investment, determine the foreign exchange available for imports.

As to imports, those of nonfactor services are exogenous. Imports of rice, consumption, and capital goods are determined as the difference between domestic demand and production. The difference between the foreign exchange available and these imports is then available for importing intermediate goods.

As to intermediate imports, the demand for them (at constant prices) is determined as a function of value-added manufacturing, the GDP deflator, and the import price in U.S. dollars. The availability of intermediate imports is determined on the basis of residual foreign exchange. The domestic price of imports is then calculated as a function of value-added manufacturing, the GDP deflator, and the availability of imported intermediate goods. The demand and supply of intermediate goods (at current prices) are then brought into balance by changes in exchange rates, tariffs, or both. The total demand and supply of intermediate goods in the economy are balanced by an implicit import-substitution effect. The identity that maintains the balance is:

$$\text{Domestic production} + \text{imports} = \text{domestic demand} + \text{import substitution.}$$

It is assumed that import substitution is limited to 20 percent of domestic demand. If the shortfall is greater than 20 percent the propensity in the economy to save is reduced, and hence demand for intermediate goods goes down because of a decline in the GDP growth rate.

The Capital Transaction Block and the Population Block

Net public transfers, taken from a submodel of the external debt situation in Indonesia (see Appendix C), are made exogenous in this model.

The population block has been treated separately and has been solved by another submodel. In this submodel population has been estimated for every year of age, separately for males and females, and for outer islands and Java. "Working population" has been defined as men between 15 and 64 years and women between 15 and 49 years. Three major assumptions have been tried: with high fertility and low mortality; low fertility and high mortality; and high fertility and high mortality (see Tables E6, E7, E8 in Appendix E). "Working population" and "dependency ratio" have been injected into the main model as exogenous variables. Participation rates among the working population has been assumed to be 72 percent of the total.

3

Functional Forms of the Model

An overview of the functional relations between dependent variables and independent explanatory variables, is given as a flow chart in Figure 8, in which triangles represent exogenous variables, boxes represent endogenous variables as vectors, and arrows represent causal sequences. Arrows in both directions suggest simultaneity. The recursive nature of the relations are taken care of by introducing time lags.

The symbols are explained as follows:

Symbol	*Definition*	*Symbol*	*Definition*
CAPMRK	Capital market	*GR*	Government current revenue
CHR	Changes in foreign exchange reserves	*GS*	Government saving
CI	Corporate income	*HE*	Household disposable income (=household expenditure)
C/O	Capital-output ratio		
CS	Corporate saving		
EXR	Nominal exchange rates	*HI*	Household income (size distribution)
FS	Foreign saving		
GC	Government current consumption	*HS*	Household saving
		IC	Intermediate consumption

Symbol	*Definition*	*Symbol*	*Definition*
LABMAR	Labor market	*PRICE*	Commodity prices
LFOR	Working population	*TC*	Total consumption
		TE	Total exports
MONEY	Money demand and money supply	*TI*	Total investment
		TIm	Total imports
		TM	Terms matrix
NEWCOM	Net commitments	*TO*	Total gross output
NR	Natural resources	*TS*	Total supply
NT	Net transfer	*TTADJ*	Terms of trade gains
PM	Import price		
POP	Population	*VA*	Value added
PR	Participation rates (working population to total population)	*W*	Wage rates
		WD	World demand
		WP	World price for exports
PRCON	Household consumption		

Total output (*TO*) determines value added (*VA*). Value added determines household income (*HI*) and corporate income (*CI*). Household income contributes to government revenue (*GR*) and to household expenditure (*HE*) and household saving (*HS*). Household expenditure determines private consumption vector (*PRCON*). Similarly, government revenue is spent on government consumption (*GC*, which includes transfer payments) and government saving (*GS*). Total consumption (*TC*) is fed by intermediate consumption (*IC*) and by *PRCON* and *GC*. Total investment (*TI*) is fed by corporate saving (*CS*), government saving (*GS*), household saving (*HS*) and foreign saving (*FS*). Total export (*TE*) is determined by world demand (*WD*) and world price (*WP*); price of imports (*PM*) and *WP* determine terms of trade changes (*TTADJ*). *TTADJ* goes to augment both corporate and personal income. Total imports (*TIm*) add to total output (*TO*) to generate total supply (*TS*). Population (*POP*), through age structure and participation rates (*PR*), determine labor supply (*LFOR*). Wage (*W*) is determined by labor market (*LABMAR*): that is, by unemployment rate and labor institutions and by cost of living changes. Wage goes to value added as wage share to GDP.

A fuller explanation of the variables and the equation systems is given in Appendix B.

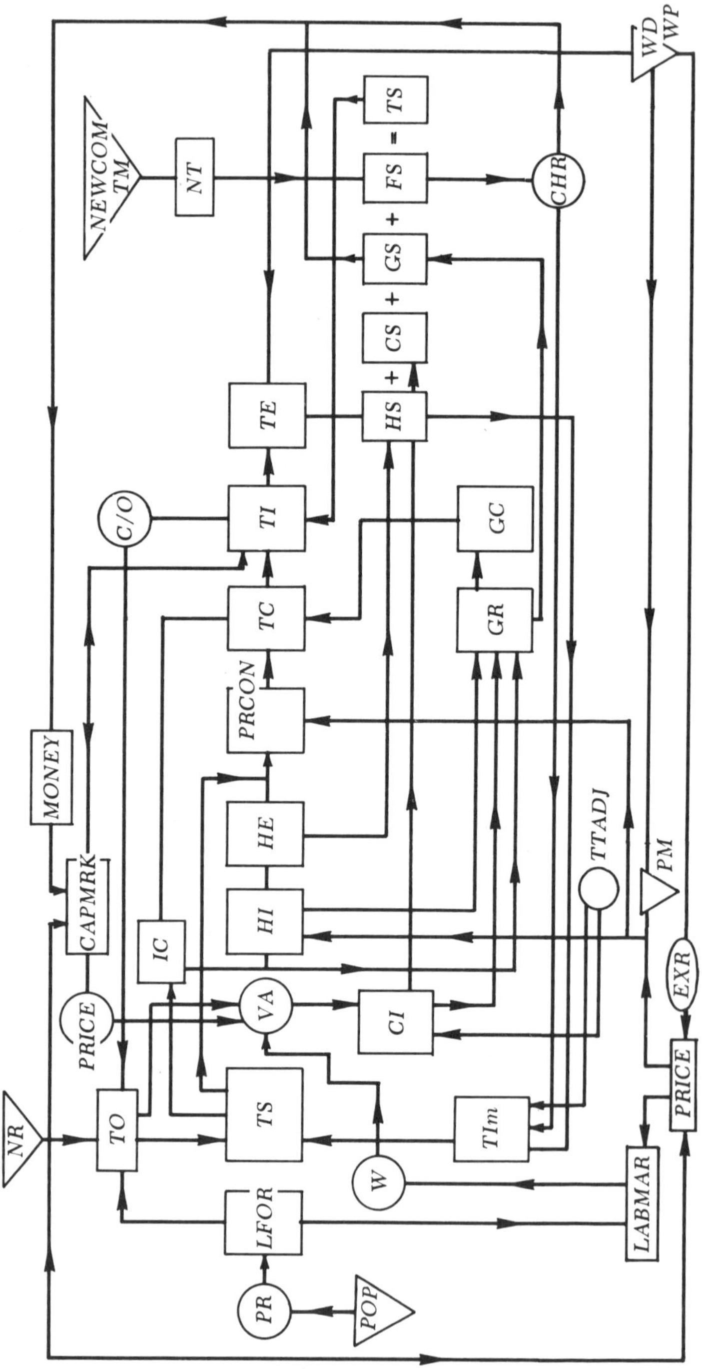

Figure 8. Flow Chart of the Indonesian Model

4

Estimation of Parameters

THIS CHAPTER PRESENTS THE METHODS used to estimate the parameters of the model. The first section discusses the relation between inputs in various sectors of production and the output realized. Other sections consider the determinants of demand as well as of imports and exports, and the elasticities of expenditure and employment. Also presented is the way in which the model deals with income distribution.

Production Functions

Rice output has been separated into that from irrigated and from nonirrigated land. On irrigated land rice production depends mainly on the irrigation and fertilizer. The two dependent variables seem to be correlated reasonably well with the two explanatory variables. The following two equations are estimated over a sample period 1960–72: [1]

$$\text{Log output rice (irrigated area)} = \underset{(3.493)}{6.926} + \underset{(7.821)}{1.872}\,\text{log area (irrigated)} + \underset{(1.679)}{0.0584}\,\text{log fertilizer}$$

$\bar{R}^2 = 0.8800$; Durbin-Watson statistic $= 1.6582$.

$$\text{Log output rice (nonirrigated)} = \underset{(3.6224)}{-2.877} + \underset{(6.0809)}{0.6602}\,\text{log area (nonirrigated)}$$

$\bar{R}^2 = 0.8451$; Durbin-Watson statistic $= 2.175$.

1. Figures in parentheses are t-statistics.

Tree crops have been regressed on area cultivated. The estimated equation is as follows:

$$\text{Log value added export crop} = \underset{(-2.538)}{-4.66} + \underset{(4.5868)}{0.998} \text{ log area tree crop}$$

$\bar{R}^2 = 0.6456$; Durbin-Watson statistic $= 0.9735$.

Output of "other agriculture" (excluding rice, tree crops, and vegetables) depends on area and a time trend, suggesting a productivity improvement over the sample period.

$$\text{Log value added of other agriculture} = \underset{(86.67)}{0.5111} \text{ log area} + \underset{(3.121)}{0.088} \text{ log time trend (1973–74)}$$

$\bar{R}^2 = 0.450$; Durbin-Watson statistic $= 1.1533$.

The production functions for remaining sectors have been decomposed into two parts, capital coefficients and labor coefficients. In all cases, a fixed marginal capital-output ratio and a fixed elasticity of labor relative to output have been assumed.

The marginal capital-output ratios for rice, tree crops, other agriculture, livestock, forestry, and fishing have been estimated from the output and investment figures given exogenously by the sector specialists, whereas marginal capital-output ratios for the manufacturing sector have been estimated again on the basis of investment and output estimates of the industry experts. The gestation lag of investments for capital goods, consumption goods (capital intensive), and intermediate goods industries have been assumed to be three years, and for consumption goods (labor intensive), two years. The capital-output ratios for capital and intermediate goods industries are placed at 4.0; for consumption goods (capital intensive), at 2.7; and for consumption goods (labor intensive), at 2.5. The lag structures have been estimated roughly from a study made by the foreign and domestic investment board in Indonesia.[2]

The capital-output ratios for trade, services, transport, public administration, banking, and mining are borrowed from different sources, including cross-country comparisons.[3]

2. An unpublished, restricted circulation document made available by the Indonesian government to a World Bank mission in 1973.

3. Republic of Indonesia, "The First Five-Year Development Plan" and "The Second Five-Year Development Plan" (Jakarta: Department of Information, n.d.) and *Pendapatan Nasional Indonesia* (National income of Indonesia), 1960–68 and 1971–74 (Jakarta: Central Bureau of Statistics, 1970 and 1975).

Demand Functions

The demand elasticities for goods and services in different sectors have been estimated by two distinctly different methods. For fish, animal husbandry, rice, and vegetables they are estimated for different income groups, for rural and urban areas separately, and for the rural and urban total from a family budget survey of 1969 conducted by the Central Bureau of Statistics in Indonesia.[4] This method of estimation will be discussed under "Expenditure Balance" below.

The demand elasticity for manufactured consumption goods has been estimated for the economy as a whole, again from the same source, as well as for lower- and higher-income groups separately. A breakdown between different manufactured items was not possible because of the problem of matching expenditure classifications with the production classifications used in the model.

The demand for intermediate goods is determined either by the input coefficient given in the input-output tables for Indonesia [5] or by the main elasticities for trade, transport, services, banking, and public administration, which are derived from time series data in the national income accounts. The demand for construction has been estimated on the basis of construction components and value-added components of capital formation in different sectors of the economy.

Tax Functions

Estimates of tax parameters for income, consumption, export and import taxes, and nontax revenues have been made from a sample study in Indonesia, done in collaboration with the International Monetary Fund, covering the seven years 1967–73. The equations used are given in Table E3 in Appendix E.

Import Functions

The import block has been divided into three groups: capital goods imports, intermediate goods imports, and consumption goods imports.

4. Republic of Indonesia, *Survey Sosial Ekonomi Nasional* (National socio-economic survey), October–December 1969 (Jakarta: Central Bureau of Statistics, 1972).

5. Tables E1 and E2 in Appendix E.

Capital goods imports are estimated on a residual basis, which measures the difference between demand for capital goods and the domestic output of the capital goods sector. The demand for capital goods depends on the machinery component in the total capital formation. Hence, it will be affected by the industry mix and by the technological changes (principally by those of capital and labor intensity). Technology changes are made exogenous in the model.

Intermediate goods imports are treated from two different angles. First, the demand for intermediate goods imports is a function of the domestic output in the manufacture sector and the price differences between domestic and foreign sources. Second, the supply of intermediate goods imports is a residual, after the available foreign exchange earnings are used up in buying capital and consumption goods.

The import price is made endogenous, to bring an equilibrium between demand for, and supply of, imports of intermediate goods. Since the world prices of imported goods at foreign currency (U.S. dollars) are exogenous, the above relations treat exchange rates as endogenous. The demand equation for intermediate imports is estimated on the basis of time series data for 1967–73, at 1973 prices:

$$\begin{aligned}\text{Log intermediate imports} = & -0.47 \\ & + \underset{(4.630)}{1.008} \text{ log value added manufacturing} \\ & + \underset{(8.089)}{2.776} \text{ log (GDP deflator/import deflator)}\end{aligned}$$

$\bar{R}^2 = 0.9948$; Durbin-Watson statistic $= 1.625$; Standard deviation $= 0.0396$.

Consumption goods imports are also estimated residually. The demand for consumption goods (manufactured), excluding rice, is estimated as a function of the level of income, from cross-section data (1969 family budget survey). The output of consumption goods is based on a supply constraint: in other words, it depends on the investment level. The difference between demand and supply gives the import of consumption goods. This import has not been found to be significantly price sensitive in the past.

Export Functions

Exports have been divided into six groups: oil, tree crops, fishing and animal husbandry, hard minerals, manufacturing, and forestry.

Exports of forestry and hard minerals are estimated on a residual basis, with domestic consumption subtracted from domestic output. Exports of oil[6] and manufacturing are demand oriented and are exogenous in the model.

Employment Functions

The employment elasticities were estimated for ten groups in order to match the 1971 census classifications. The 1971 value added per capita was estimated for each group and then adjusted by price and productivity changes to update them to the 1973 base. Most of the employment elasticities are borrowed from the plan document.[7] Independent changes have been made by employment experts to impart a rough notion of feasibility to these figures. These assumptions of employment elasticities obviously carry an assumption regarding changes in labor productivity measured as output per worker.

For public works, employment has been estimated on the assumption of a fixed per capita income. For minerals, including oil, employment is set endogenously as a percentage of the total labor force.

Income Distribution

The model treats the income distribution in a rather novel way. For simulating the income distribution, sectoral income distribution data are needed at the base period, but this information was not available for each output sector in Indonesia. There was, however, an expenditure study for 32,000 households for the rural and urban sectors, made in 1969.[8] This expenditure study also has income information, but it is not very reliable. (From the experience of other countries, it is known that any information regarding income is quite imprecise.) Nevertheless, a good knowledge of the initial sectoral income distribution was necessary for computing the income distribution in the model, so the 1971 census data were used to arrive at this distribution.

6. Treated as net: that is, after subtracting the imports of the oil sector.
7. Republic of Indonesia, "The Second Five-Year Development Plan."
8. *Survey Sosial Ekonomi Nasional.*

The 1971 census contains information about regional productivity differences for each sector. Assuming a relation between employed and total population, an initial regional income distribution can be estimated for each sector.

The income differences of any sector have three components: regional differences, differences within a region (as inequality between income classes), and overlap of income of different regions. In the estimation of sectoral inequality, it has been assumed that the income distribution of any sector within a region is spread by a density function, as given by a smoothening process in a continuous sense as if plotted on a graph. It was assumed that the income pattern within a sector of a region was spread over a narrow range, as given between two points of observation drawn in a graph. This assumption obviously introduces a downward bias in the estimation of income inequality for any sector.[9] An attempt was made, however, to avoid this bias by estimating only the index of inequality intertemporally—that is, relative changes in income inequality—assuming that the bias remains the same over time. But the present estimate is very close to the Gini inequality derived from the family expenditure study of 1969.

As to the agricultural sector, information was available regarding land distribution. In the present exercise, the concentration coefficient of land distribution derived from the above information is almost the same as the one estimated for agriculture on the basis of a regional study.[10]

For the ten sectors—agriculture, small-scale industry, large-scale industry, construction, electricity and power, transport, trade, banking, public administration and defense, and services—the average productivity and the employed labor force have been tabulated for each of the twenty-six regions of Indonesia.[11] Table 1 gives average

9. The overlap of income component was ignored when the Gini coefficient was calculated.

10. Sri Edi Swasono, Hendra Esmara, and others, *Perhitungan Pendapatan Regional Di Indonesia* (Regional income in Indonesia), 1968–72, 3 vols. (Jakarta: Planning Commission, 1974).

11. The regions are East Java, Central Java, West Java, Special Capital Territory Jakarta, Special Territory Yogyakata, North Sumatra, Jambi, Riau, West Sumatra, South Sumatra, Lampung, Special Territory Aceh, Bengkulu, West Kalimantan, East Kalimantan, South Kalimantan, Central Kalimantan, South Sulawesi, Central Sulawesi, Southeast Sulawesi, North Sulawesi, Maluku, Bali, West Nusa Tenggara, East Nusa Tenggara, and Irian Jaya.

income in the first column and population in the second column. They have been arranged in ascending order. Gini coefficients (or income concentration) are estimated for each sector. They are as follows:

Agriculture, 0.417
Small-scale industry, 0.384
Large-scale industry, 0.242
Construction, 0.276
Electricity and power, 0.342
Transport, 0.341
Trade, 0.209
Banking, 0.293
Public administration and defense, 0.155
Services, 0.240
Economy (as a whole), 0.377

Comparable statistics from Malaysia give an income concentration of 0.36 in 1958–59 and 0.48 in 1970. This suggests that the estimates for Indonesia have some statistical bias, which must have been introduced through an underestimation of intrasector income distribution within a region. In a further simulation, an attempt was made to calculate the income inequality in the disposable income of 1973. This Gini coefficient was 0.407, which suggests a regressiveness in the tax system, principally because of the distribution of the incidence of indirect taxes. The expenditure coefficient, derived from the household survey, shows an income concentration of 0.345.

Money Functions

Money demand and money supply have been estimated on the basis of time series data spreading over the period 1960–61 to 1973–74: [12]

$$\text{Log}\left(\frac{M_t}{P_t}\right) = -0.370 + 0.729 \log \frac{M_{t-1}}{P_{t-1}} + 0.539 \log Y - 0.518\,\pi,$$
$$(-3.0) \qquad (11.6) \qquad (3.2) \qquad -(5.80)$$

$\bar{R}^2 = 0.992$; Durbin-Watson statistic $= 2.3116$.

$$M_t = 1.18\, RM_t, \text{ and}$$
$$RM_t = G_t - T_t + H_t$$

where P_t is the price index,
M_t is the narrow money,
Y_t is the real output,
RM_t is the reserve money,
π is the inflation rate $(\Delta P_t / P_{t-1})$,

12. Bijan B. Aghevli, "An Economic Model of the Money Sector for Indonesia," International Monetary Fund, restricted circulation document, 1975.

Table 1. Average Income and Population in Indonesia in All Sectors, by

Agriculture		*Mining*		*Small-scale industry*		*Large-scale industry*	
Income	*Population*	*Income*	*Population*	*Income*	*Population*	*Income*	*Population*
659	626,353	—	267	587	9,545	118	143,716
2,973	803,549	—	64	1,572	764	899	6,236
3,854	485,212	—	990	2,722	5,087	1,406	58,463
3,984	574,310	—	131	6,274	153,416	1,728	51,326
4,119	509,653	—	279	7,276	3,300	2,116	37,263
4,391	722,864	—	3,531	8,497	1,444	2,504	688,614
5,021	203,313	—	209	11,392	3,794	2,895	19,985
5,207	243,762	—	590	12,068	2,321	3,727	86,142
5,547	3,880,970	—	92	14,318	117,060	4,494	371,384
5,586	6,503,136	—	50	15,582	1,659	5,161	387,980
5,614	740,693	—	88	16,052	18,167	5,261	1,115
6,237	488,716	—	4,628	18,567	24,974	5,506	13,000
6,343	160,486	—	7,255	18,654	19,709	6,432	24,296
6,586	49,346	—	4,402	19,673	5,940	6,710	6,270
6,882	849,640	—	591	21,561	6,558	7,213	14,587
7,268	1,691,677	—	84	22,571	4,882	7,395	34,315
7,297	410,652	—	3,023	23,976	679	9,066	13,265
7,597	936,117	—	3,925	26,042	10,286	10,307	18,938
8,652	338,112	—	1,995	28,166	578	12,028	7,099
9,541	276,865	228	7,863	34,326	5,122	12,261	2,539
10,547	234,757	279	215	38,598	129,682	12,668	49,327
10,914	366,091	674	1,960	53,396	2,883	17,735	17,617
19,304	166,087	13,782	12,274	75,504	23,622	25,728	9,863
74,404	133,057	27,329	26,101	80,201	70,708	53,067	1,839
93,090	481,054	157,708	1,754	81,286	2,652	0	0
98,156	11,445	0	0	123,158	1,941	0	0

—Negligible.
Source: Sri Edi Swasono, Hendra Esmara, and others, *Perhitungan Pendapatan Regional Di Indonesia* (Regional income in Indonesia), 1968–72, 3 vols. (Jakarta: Planning Commission, 1974).

G_t is the government expenditure,

T_t is the government revenue (constant), and

H_t is the residual including the private sector's balance of payments minus public foreign expenditures, plus net claims of the Central Bank on the nongovernment sector.

Expenditure Balance

The expenditure elasticities for rice, vegetables, fish, and meat have been estimated by econometric estimation by the double log rela-

Region (in Ascending Order), 1971

Construction		Electricity and power		Transport		Trade	
Income	Population	Income	Population	Income	Population	Income	Population
1,467	2,180	172	93	1,644	2,219	2,776	48,937
1,486	3,193	825	80	3,622	6,709	3,715	21,651
2,486	1,286	1,378	656	7,396	4,659	5,609	131,030
10,472	121,764	3,632	1,038	7,631	8,852	6,158	72,633
10,491	18,165	3,985	334	8,166	11,007	7,574	77,020
12,617	18,247	6,812	7,991	8,775	12,066	8,807	1,009,978
13,234	9,568	10,565	124	9,203	189,054	9,072	317,936
15,674	151,617	11,338	71	9,378	15,635	11,486	6,557
15,796	14,498	12,135	623	9,535	131,317	11,974	812,231
16,461	113,521	21,975	471	11,509	43,105	12,105	78,362
17,936	5,277	22,568	444	12,838	15,234	13,572	110,886
18,947	13,771	24,568	1,261	13,107	1,661	14,703	1,089,170
19,668	6,048	31,435	2,564	13,448	187,983	18,443	56,181
20,035	8,682	35,468	278	14,664	64,369	22,979	40,664
22,661	13,602	35,918	4,971	15,615	19,820	24,778	26,076
24,034	8,887	36,057	346	17,223	5,376	26,306	96,427
24,216	23,239	40,116	86	19,569	7,725	27,419	9,415
25,791	92,141	41,276	486	20,358	138,003	28,564	10,008
26,129	2,741	44,334	7,595	21,649	7,815	37,312	10,031
29,459	31,737	44,255	141	26,267	11,327	38,092	4,906
30,807	7,579	45,217	138	28,282	10,016	40,555	143,525
31,001	1,279	53,338	767	32,478	8,762	42,762	22,368
32,594	2,433	56,903	6,286	36,057	1,367	54,771	3,737
33,801	2,573	64,553	369	40,510	2,979	78,117	7,473
39,432	4,016	73,333	9	57,423	30,296	119,737	39,362
210,058	3,428	121,095	137	140,474	14,098	160,695	14,997

(*Table continues on the following page.*)

tions from grouped data[13] and by graphical method. The first assumes a constant elasticity of demand for all income classes. The second gives different elasticity for different income classes. Because it was desirable to emphasize the impact of changes in income distribution on the demand pattern and growth over a long time horizon, the second method was chosen. For this purpose four expenditure classes were established: Rp0–1,000 per capita per month, Rp1,001–2,000, Rp2,001–4,000, and Rp4,001 and above. The data are based on the national family budget survey of 1969.[14] The

13. N. Kakwani and N. Podder, "Efficient Estimates of the Lorenz Curve and Associated Inequality Measures from Grouped Observations," World Bank, Development Research Center, Discussion Paper no. 10, restricted circulation document, 1975.

14. *Survey Sosial Ekonomi Nasional.*

Table 1 (*continued*)

Banking		*Public administration and defense*		*Services*	
Income	*Population*	*Income*	*Population*	*Income*	*Population*
3,156	45	156	10,385	2,987	13,397
13,028	393	2,747	153,858	3,328	11,835
14,574	1,209	3,434	11,009	3,652	136,908
15,895	155	6,577	45,734	3,937	42,267
21,589	127	7,452	30,010	3,996	101,078
25,984	217	8,235	494,717	3,997	203,477
27,037	1,212	9,416	33,687	4,062	60,599
27,530	33	10,652	35,174	4,105	58,562
32,729	1,081	11,306	16,120	4,240	692,702
33,105	1,311	12,399	142,520	4,269	935,279
37,335	2,341	12,789	63,685	4,311	15,707
38,060	730	13,645	38,711	4,384	26,450
38,191	12,215	14,005	37,478	4,388	91,039
39,865	74	14,534	36,647	4,459	92,073
41,073	1,048	14,536	10,151	4,463	456,558
49,871	465	14,705	360,843	4,525	24,749
62,835	3,646	15,618	11,801	4,570	762,247
68,255	118	16,343	32,635	4,676	59,121
69,987	75	16,516	34,956	4,685	56,807
72,566	33	16,595	18,747	4,767	26,789
78,559	22	22,672	32,511	4,800	710
80,506	122	23,016	61,854	4,945	66,255
83,580	98	25,204	131,496	4,974	49,161
89,833	35	36,285	15,619	5,278	27,421
91,531	49	38,508	15,051	9,914	28,800
121,914	16	100,936	2,800	16,021	19,833

—Negligible.
Source: Sri Edi Swasono, Hendra Esmara, and others *Perhitungan Pendapatan Regional Di Indonesia* (Regional income in Indonesia), 1968–72, 3 vols. (Jakarta: Planning Commission, 1974).

marginal coefficients for each class have been estimated as follows, in percentage:

Item consumed	*1*	*2*	*3*	*4*
Rice	40	20	9	−2.5
Fish	7	8	7.5	5
Meat	5	10	12	9
Vegetables	14	15.5	16.5	17.5

The elasticity of consumption for each class has been estimated by multiplying the marginal coefficient in each class by the ratio of total expenditures to the total consumption of each class. The estimated parameters are presented in Appendix B.

5

Alternative Simulation Plans and Testing of Hypotheses

To TEST EMPIRICALLY the alternative hypotheses on growth, equity, poverty, and employment, developed in Chapter 1, several policy variables and parameters have been specified to trace the alternative simulation paths of the economy:

Policy-type variables

—Changes in foreign exchange reserves affecting net capital inflow
—Intended investments by changing cost of investments (or money supply) or direct intervention
—Investments in rural development
—Oil revenue, or taxes
—Government expenditures
—Government subsidies
—Nominal profit rates
—Participation rates and working population (that is, dependency ratio)
—Rate of increase of irrigation in rice
—Rate of increase of fertilizer in rice
—Rate of increase of area under tree crops and other agriculture

Policy-type parameters

—Investment allocation parameters
—Tax rates: direct, indirect, and on exports and imports
—Subsidies
—Price relatives by means of tax or subsidy

—Exchange rate changes
—Wage policy by means of wage bargaining or changes in labor income

In addition, three other nonpolicy variables have been specified:

—Fertility and mortality rate
—World price changes
—Exports of oil

A possible development strategy for Indonesia in light of the findings is discussed later in this chapter.

Computer Simulations

The following alternative sensitivity analysis has been performed with the help of the present model.

Alternative I. The basic run involved a projection model with a maximum number of functional relations derived from the past. For detailed inputs, see Appendixes A and B. The other alternatives have been described as follows by presenting only the changes from the basic run.

Alternative II. In this, an income transfer policy improves equity by taxing the rich and paying the poor. The richest class has been taxed Rp100 thousand million in 1973; this figure increases by 10 percent a year thereafter. The receipts are distributed equally among the three lower income classes.

Alternative III. Investment in rural development is reduced to zero and the growth of the agriculture sector has been lowered from 6.5 percent to approximately 5 percent a year. Taxes have been increased by Rp20 thousand million in 1973 and 15 percent thereafter and government expenditure has been reduced by Rp100 thousand million and 15 percent thereafter.

Alternative IV. A wage policy stipulates a minimum growth of real income of the wage earners, 2 percent a year above their normal changes.

Alternative V. This provides for a cash reserve policy changing net capital inflow from abroad, which has been increased by 10 percent a year from the present level.

Alternative VI. A development strategy emphasizes industry, as opposed to agriculture. For this purpose, the rural development program has been reduced by half and agriculture growth has been reduced from 6.5 percent to 6 percent a year.

Alternative VII. This involves an increase in public saving by increasing government revenue (through direct taxes) and decreasing government expenditure, starting from alternative VI. Taxes are increased by Rp20 thousand million in 1973 and 15 percent a year thereafter, and public expenditure is reduced by Rp100 thousand million and 15 percent thereafter.

Alternative VIII. In this, public saving is decreased by increasing government expenditure and decreasing government revenue, starting from alternative VI. Taxes are decreased by Rp20 thousand million in 1974 and 15 percent a year thereafter, and expenditure is increased by Rp100 thousand million in 1974 and 15 percent a year thereafter.

Alternative IX. This involves reduced population growth: that is, same growth of the working population but lower growth of the population as a whole. The participation rate thereby has been reduced to that of 1972.

Alternative X. The price index of primary goods in the foreign market is increased. Prices are raised for food, tree crops, and oil.

Alternative XI. Different combinations of fertility and mortality and their impact over a longer time horizon (1974–97): XI(a) low mortality–low fertility, XI(b) high mortality–high fertility, XI(c) low mortality–high fertility.

Alternative XII. This is the same as alternative III, but government expenditure is increased to the level of the government revenue (a balanced-budget concept). The increase in government expenditure is confined to public consumption only and not to transfer payment, to make it a distribution-neutral measure.

Alternative XIII. This is the same as alternative III, but government expenditure is doubled. Again, additional expenditure is confined to public consumption only.

Alternative XIV(a). This is the same as alternative III, but government revenue is raised by doubling the indirect tax rates.

Alternative XIV(b). This is the same as alternative III, but government revenue is raised by increasing direct tax receipts by the same amount of the indirect tax receipts from the highest income class, as in alternative XIV(a).

Alternative XV(a). This is the same as alternative XIV(b), but

Table 2. Economic Indicators of Projected Growth under Alternative Distributive-Neutral Policies

Indicator	Base 1973	Alternatives: XII 1980	XII 1985	XIII 1980	XIII 1985	III 1980	III 1985	XIV(a) 1980	XIV(a) 1985
GDP (thousand millions of rupiahs at 1973 market price)	6,163	8,546	11,146	10,014	14,326	11,185	18,174	11,951	21,107
GDP annual percentage change (base 1973)	—	4.8	5.1	7.2	7.3	8.9	9.4	9.9	10.8
Income distribution (Gini coefficient)	0.45	0.568	0.680	0.562	0.640	0.551	0.606	0.548	0.585
Unemployment (percent)	6.8	15.2	19.4	11.6	13.7	9.0	8.0	7.6	4.5
Poverty index	0.56	0.78	0.88	0.73	0.82	0.67	0.71	0.65	0.62
Exchange rate (rupiahs to US$1.00)	415	339	318	390	387	427	475	451	493
GDP deflator	100	232	345	234	333	238	359	239	367
Input substitution (percent)	—[a]	—[a]	—[a]	—[a]	—[a]	{20}		{29}	
Public saving (thousand millions of rupiahs, 1973 price)	4.2	0	0	6.9	6.8	12.3	13.4	15.4	18.3
Gross investment (thousand millions of rupiahs, 1973 price)	19.0	16.0	16.4	22.6	22.3	28.1	29.1	33.8	36.9
Per capita income (rupiahs)	48,600	57,100	66,600	66,900	85,600	74,700	108,600	79,800	126,100

a. No substitution.

investment in rural development and agriculture have been raised to the level of the basic run, alternative I.

Alternative XV(b). This is the same as alternative XV(a), but it includes an income-redistribution policy. The wage and nonwage incomes in each sector have been raised in proportion to the increase of value added per laborer. This essentially means a heavy shift of income from nonwage earners (the higher income class) to wage earners (the lower income class).

Alternative XV(c). This is the same as alternative XV(b), but with a lower labor absorption in the public sector (as in the World Bank Economic Report).[1]

Alternative XVI(a). This is the same as alternative III, but agriculture growth and expenses for rural development have been brought back to the values of the basic solution, alternative I.

Alternative XVI(b). This is the same as alternative XVI(a), with the wage equations as in alternative XV(b).

Testing of the Hypotheses

Stage of development and equity. The alternative runs in Table 2 confined to distributive neutral policies, indicate that income inequality will increase over time, with a corresponding increase in GDP per capita. But because the per capita income in Indonesia is very low, it may be presumed that the functional relation between equity and per capita income refers to the region on the left of point *B'* in Figure 2. This proves the hypothesis about stages of development and equity stated in Chapter 1, subject to the assumption that no drastic redistributive policies are used.

Growth and equity. To test the hypothesis about growth and equity, only those alternatives were selected which would satisfy the conditions of a distributive-neutral policy: alternatives III, XII, XIII, and XIV(a). The differences between these four alternatives lie in their assumption regarding different levels of public savings generated in the economy by fiscal measures that ensure neutrality on the distributive front. It is assumed also that additional public saving will be invested by the same allocation principle in all the alternative runs—and without any positive distributive implications (such as expenditure on social sectors). The additional saving will

1. "Indonesia: Development Prospects and Needs," World Bank Economic Report no. 708 IND, April 15, 1975, restricted circulation document.

Table 3. Selected Economic Indicators of Projected Growth and Equity under Alternative Development Strategies

Indicator	Alternative and type									
	XIV (a), distributive neutral		*XIV (b), redistributive*		*XV(a), redistributive (sector mix)*		*XIV (a), distributive neutral*		*XIV (b), redistributive*	
	1980	*1985*	*1980*	*1985*	*1980*	*1985*	*1980*	*1985*	*1980*	*1985*
GDP annual percentage change (base 1973)	9.9	10.8	9.4	10.1	9.8	10.5	8.8	8.9	8.7	8.6
Income distribution (Gini coefficient)	0.548	0.585	0.500	0.524	0.509	0.526	0.511	0.545	0.371	0.351
Unemployment (percent)	7.6	4.5	5.2	0.9	4.3	0	5.7	3.5	5.5	3.7
Public savings (as a percent of GDP)	15.3	18.3	15.1	18.4	14.9	24.0	11.7	13.0	11.9	12.9
Gross investment	33.8	36.9	33.0	36.0	32.9	36.7	27.4	28.2	26.2	32.1

be generated either by a general sales tax (of equal percentage) applicable to all goods or by reducing public consumption, which will have no discriminating impact on any specific income class. The four alternatives are presented in Table 2.

For the year 1985, alternative XII gives the lowest growth rate—5.1 percent a year between 1973 and 1985—but at the same time the highest income inequality (measured by the Gini coefficient), 0.680 in 1985. Alternative XIV gives for the same year a higher growth rate, 10.8 percent a year between 1973 and 1985, but a lower income inequality, 0.585. In fact, all the alternatives consistently show that for all years (of which only 1980 and 1985 have been recorded in the table) growth and equity are positively related. This supports the hypothesis described in Chapter 1.

Growth with equity. This hypothesis has been tested in two different approaches. In the first, those alternative sensitivity runs were selected which show strict contrast in their development strategies: (a) growth without redistributive policy and (b) growth with redistributive policy. In the second approach a large number of cases were selected in which different redistributive measures are adopted from a base configuration. Rank correlation was then used to examine whether these measures are negatively correlated with growth.

The subtle differences between the two approaches are that in the first approach the growth potential of an economy is being compared against distributive-neutral and distributive-positive fiscal policies and under the same set of savings constraints; in the second approach the objective is to learn whether an increase in income equity achieved by redistributive measures will actually reduce growth.

The alternatives selected for the first approach are XIV(a), XIV(b), XV(a), XVI(a), and XVI(b). Alternative XIV(a) uses indirect taxes (general sales tax) to finance government investment, whereas XIV(b) uses direct taxes (progressive) to finance the same amount. Hence, a comparison of the growth differences between these two cases would test the hypothesis. It can be observed in Table 3 that, when redistributive measures are adopted, the growth rate declines from 10.8 percent a year to 10.1 percent over the period 1973–85, and income inequality in 1985 falls from 0.585 to 0.524.

Similarly, differences between XVI(a) and XVI(b) and between XV(a) and XV(b) reflect the effects of a drastic wage (redistributive) policy. Again, growth declines when redistribution is increased. Furthermore, the difference between XIV(a) and XV(a) lies in a changing sectoral mix of investment from industry to agriculture. This mix again results in a reduction in growth and also in income inequality.

Therefore, all the runs support the hypothesis that a policy of growth with equity exhibits a negative correlation between growth and equity.

In the second approach alternatives I, II, IV, V, VI, VII, IX, and X were selected, in all of which a positive redistributive policy had been adopted, starting from the basic run (see Table 4). Beginning with high equity and low growth, as in alternative II, different policy packages were used to determine whether growth was sacrificed in the effort to reduce income inequality.

All of the alternatives show a negative relation between the two objectives of growth and income distribution (Figure 9). An attempt has been made to estimate their association roughly by the rank correlation method. The value of this rank correlation is as high as $= -0.625$, which supports the hypothesis that growth and equity in general do conflict with one another.

Growth and employment. The relation between growth and employment is again not invariant to the policy package adopted. In the introduction it was explained that over a wide range this relation can be assumed to be positive. But empirically, when an attempt was made to estimate the nature of the correlation over several feasible alternative policies, it was found that the association was very weak, although of positive nature. (The rank correlation coefficient was as low as $+0.102$ for all the policies and rose to only $+0.367$ when alternative VI was excluded.) To put it a different way, it seems that growth and employment over a feasible policy range have no significant association (Figure 10). Hence, a specific employment policy must be treated separately from a general growth policy.

Growth and poverty. As regards poverty—defined as the standard of living below a minimum requirement level—the alternative simulations indicate that the generation of employment and the elimination of poverty are highly correlated: the rank correlation coefficient is as high as $+0.929$. This suggests that a drive against poverty must have an employment policy as a necessary tool,

Figure 9. The Negative Relation between Growth and Income under Certain Alternative Policies

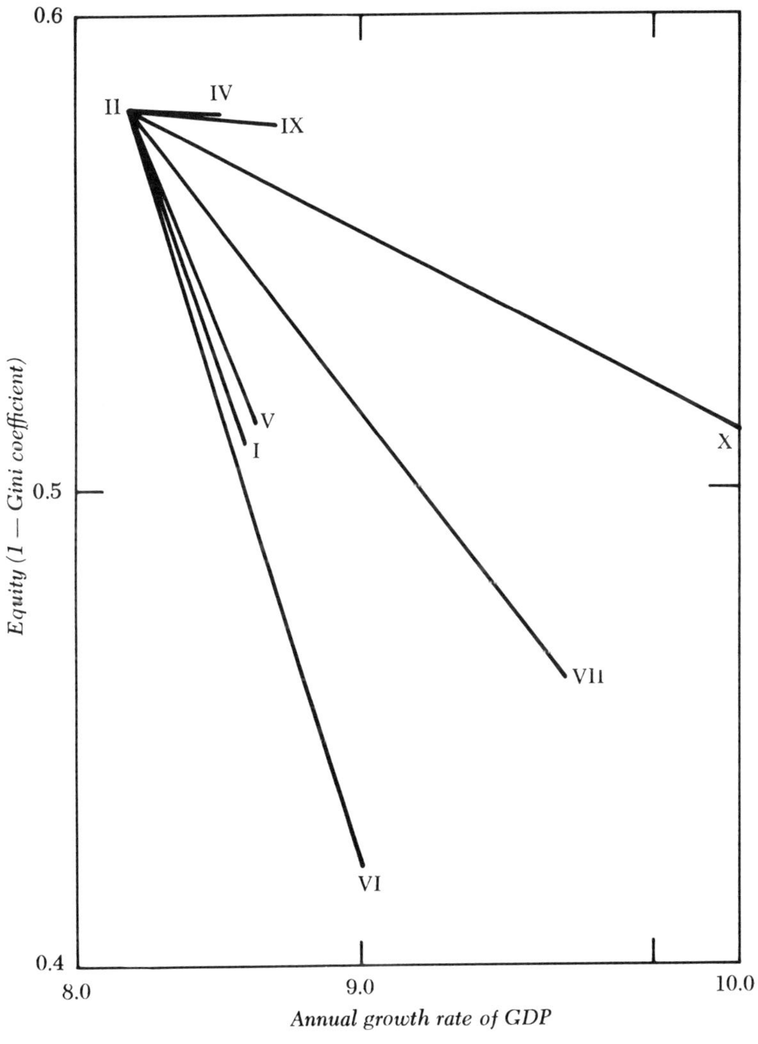

Table 4. Economic Indicators of Projected Growth and Income Inequality under Alternative Policies of Redistribution

		Alternative							
		I		*II*		*IV*		*V*	
Indicator	*Base 1973*	*1980*	*1985*	*1980*	*1985*	*1980*	*1985*	*1980*	*1985*
GDP (thousand millions of rupiahs at 1973 market price)	6,163	10,794	16,564	10,612	15,730	10,797	16,455	10,794	16,677
GDP annual percentage change (base 1973)	. . .	8.3	8.6	8.1	8.1	8.3	8.5	8.3	8.6
Income distribution (Gini coefficient)	0.450	0.491	0.495	0.420	0.418	0.450	0.422	0.491	0.495
Unemployment (percent)	6.8	4.1	0.4	4.2	1.4	3.9	0.2	4.1	0.3
Poverty index	0.730	0.525	0.268	0.144	0.319	0.441	0.014	0.525	0.257
Exchange rate (rupiahs to US$1.00)	415	499	676	507	659	503	676	500	678
GDP deflator	100	267	486	270	488	268	489	267	486
Gross investment	1,208	2,715	4,927	2,573	4,359	2,665	4,705	2,715	5,015
Per capita income (rupiahs)	48,600	72,100	99,000	70,900	94,000	74,000	98,300	72,100	99,600

Indicator	VI 1980	VI 1985	VII 1980	VII 1985	IX 1980	IX 1985	X 1980	X 1985
	Alternative							
	VI		*VII*		*IX*		*X*	
Indicator	*1980*	*1985*	*1980*	*1985*	*1980*	*1985*	*1980*	*1985*
GDP (thousand millions of rupiahs at market price)	10,971	17,338	11,395	18,460	10,803	16,766	10,713	17,518
GDP annual percentage change (base 1973)	8.6	9.0	9.2	9.7	8.3	8.7	8.2	10.3
Income distribution (Gini coefficient)	0.522	0.576	0.514	0.540	0.485	0.425	0.493	0.491
Unemployment (percent)	5.5	2.7	4.5	0.6	3.0	—0.03	4.3	—0.01
Poverty index	0.600	0.580	0.560	0.391	0.485	—0.297	0.537	0.165
Exchange rate (rupiahs to US$1.00)	1.204	1.673	1,267	1.844	1.207	1.710	1.330	2.580
GDP deflator	262	465	264	480	268	501	318	641
Gross investment	2,800	5,397	3,086	6,155	2,716	5,112	2,705	6,352
Per capita income (rupiahs)	73,300	103,600	76,100	111,400	72,200	100,200	71,600	104,700

Figure 10. The Relation between Growth and Employment under Certain Alternative Policies

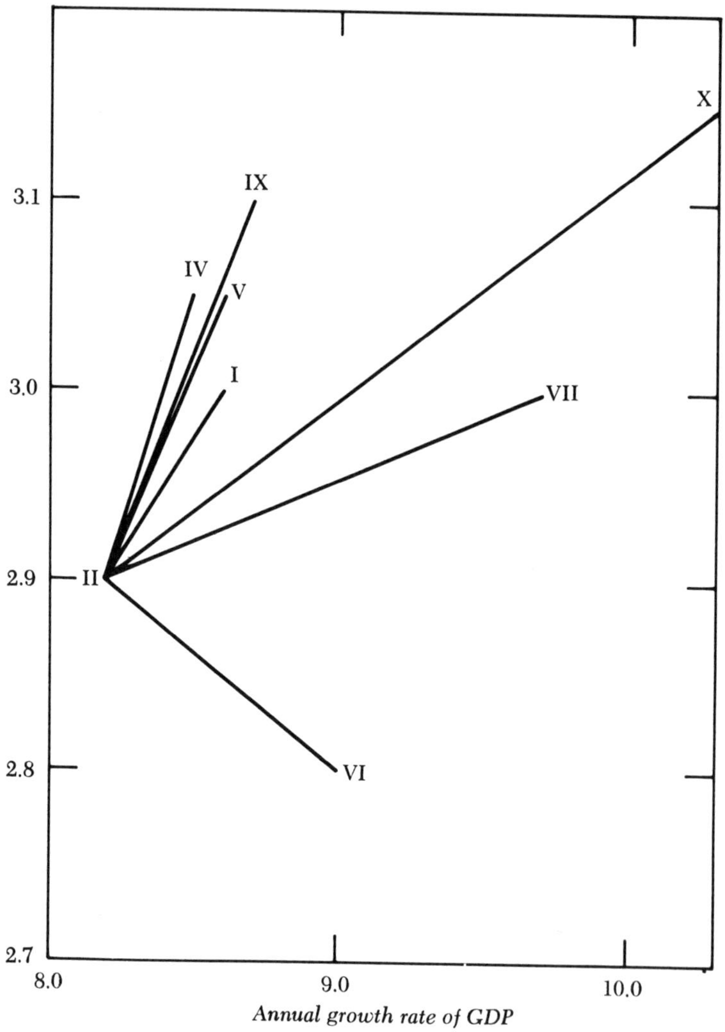

whereas output growth, employment, and income distribution are only subsidiary considerations.

The sensitivity tests regarding different population growth have been carried out in alternatives XI(a), XI(b), and XI(c). The different changes in the population do not, however, have any significant effect on growth, income distribution, or employment over the next decade: that is, by 1985. Therefore, the time horizon of the model was extended up to 1997. Changes in mortality, fertility, and participation rates under alternatives XI(a), XI(b), and XI(c) are given in Tables E6, E7, E8, in Appendix E. Population increases very slowly in alternative XI(a), whereas in alternative XI(c) it increases very fast, almost at the present high rate. In alternative XI(c) nearly 3.2 million more persons will be added to the total population by 1997, compared with alternative XI(a).

The economic and social consequences of this accelerated population growth appear to be gloomy, although perceptible only after 1985 (see Tables E9, E10, E11 in Appendix E). This growth will result in a significant decline in the rate of growth of real GDP. Unemployment, poverty, and income inequality will rise in spite of the fact that in this alternative a more labor-intensive technique was assumed. But the finding is not surprising. Increased population does result in higher consumption, lower saving, and lower average income of the wage earners and the poor. The decline in output in alternative XI(c) will be nearly Rp400 billion, or 6 percent of the GDP of 1974 at 1973 prices.

In alternative XI(a), which assumes lower population growth, full employment can be reached by 1997, whereas in alternative XI(c), which assumes higher population growth, it cannot be reached in this century. The worst effect of the higher population growth is, however, a much higher poverty index, nearly 65 percent higher in alternative XI(c) compared with alternative XI(a).

An attempt also has been made to explore the implications of a monetary policy in Indonesia for different development strategies. In general, a ratio of money expansion of 22 to 24 percent a year will be warranted in all the alternatives. The highest ratio of growth of money expansion will be warranted, in both alternative VII and alternative X. Money demand increases least, however, in the wage alternative (III) and most in the economic report case (alternative VII).

A Lesson from Hypothesis Testing

In light of the validation of the hypothesis regarding growth and income equity, two contrasting development strategies were formulated for any typical developing country. They have been presented graphically in Figure 11.

The axis 0x measures per capita income. *OTHG* measures the time scale for higher growth (with distributive-neutral policy), and *OTLGR* measures the time scale of lower growth (with redistributive policy). Three time periods are studied, 10, 20, and 30 years. E_{10}, E_{20}, and E_{30} measure income equity, observed in time T_{10}, T_{20}, and T_{30} plotted along *OTHG;* G_{10}, G_{20}, and G_{30} measure corresponding per capita incomes. Similarly, E'_{10}, E'_{20}, and E'_{30} measure equity

Figure 11. Alternative Development Strategies in the Tradeoff over Time between Growth and Equity

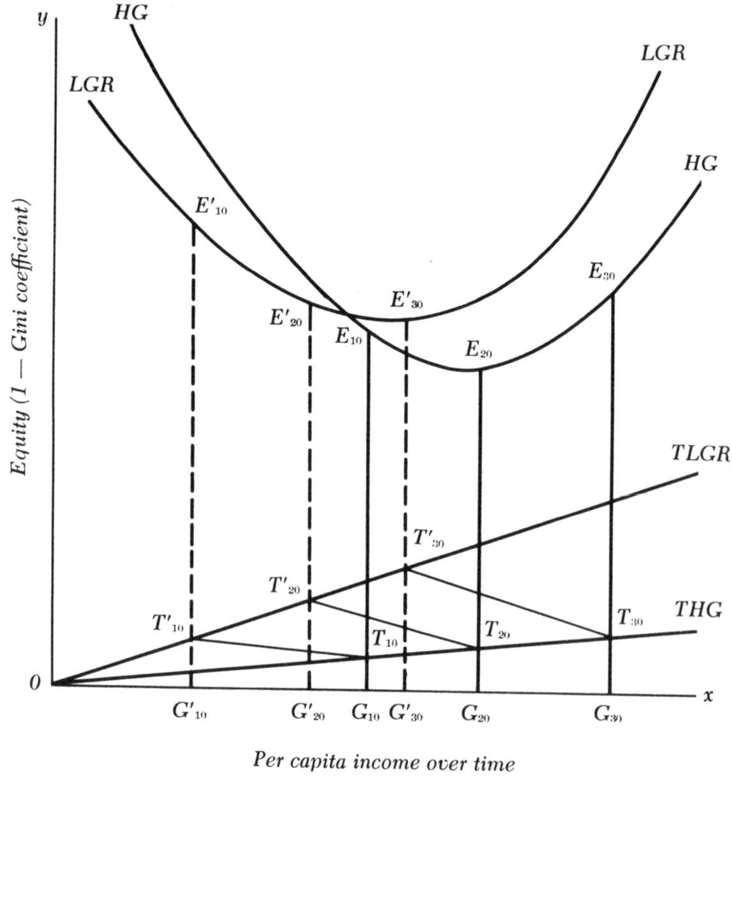

observed in time T'_{10}, T'_{20}, and T'_{30} on *OTLGR* (for redistributive policy); G'_{10}, G'_{20}, *and* G'_{30} measure corresponding per capita income.

A comparison of the two development strategies shows that at period 10, growth by means of redistributive policy measures (*LGR*) will bring about lower per capita income but higher equity compared with growth achieved through distributive-neutral policy measures (*HG*). The situation will remain the same even at period 20, but thereafter income equity will begin to improve under the second course (*HG*) but will continue deteriorating under the first (*LGR*). Finally, at period 30 the second course will bring about both higher income equity and higher per capita income.

To sum up, the second strategy in the long run is preferable on both counts—and it helps in bringing about a more rapid transition for the country. In the process of transition, however, it will raise inequality to a very high level. The alternative computer simulations with the present Indonesian model obtain only before period 20, but the above analysis brings out clearly two major development choices.

First, if a country can afford to sacrifice the need for attaining higher equity (in the short term) or if a positive income distribution policy is not feasible, a faster growth is preferable. It will expedite the period of transition from a falling to a rising equity phase, and in the long run it will give both higher per capita income and higher equity.

Second, if the country already has a very low income equity and has an immediate need for an improvement in equity—on economic, political, or social grounds—some sacrifice of growth is to be recommended to achieve improvement in income equity by positive employment and income distribution policy. Such a course would postpone the transition phase, but it would help to prevent a fall in income equity to a low level.

A choice between the two courses will evidently be country specific and will depend more on institutional factors than on economic ones. Again, in real life there will be more than two alternative courses open to an economy. The range of alternatives will depend on the policy packages used in the development process. But the basic choice between all the alternatives will be in relation to "today's gain" versus "tomorrow's gain," evaluated against the tolerance level of the country regarding income inequality.

Appendix A

Exogenous Variables for the Basic Run

	Variable number
Export value (thousand millions of 1973 rupiahs)	
Export of fishing and animal husbandry	(239)
Export of oil	(362)
Export of manufacturing	(534)
Export price index (1973=US$1.00)	
Manufacture	(435)
Tree crops	(493)
Forestry	(495)
Fish and animal husbandry	(496)
Oil	(497)
Mineral	(498)
Imports value (thousand millions of current rupiahs)	
Net import of nonfactor services	(500)
Import price index (1973=US$1.00)	
Manufacture	(491)
Food	(492)
Other balance of payments variables	
Net factor service income (thousand millions of current rupiahs)	(192)

	Variable number
Net private transfers (U.S. dollars)	(86)
Net public transfers (U.S. dollars)	(180)
Investments (thousand millions of 1973 rupiahs)	
Intended investment	(279)
Mineral	(282)
Rural development	(312)
Minico	(420)
Public finance (thousand millions of rupiahs)	
Oil revenue (current)	(321)
Government expenditure (constant)	(322)
Government subsidy (constant)	(302)
Nontax revenue (constant)	(319)
Discretionary taxes (current)	(523)
Expenditure economy (current)	(524)
Subsidies expenditure, class 1	(347)
Subsidies expenditure, class 2	(348)
Subsidies expenditure, class 3	(349)
Returns from capital	
Nominal return from capital, food	(453)
Nominal return from capital, manufacture	(456)
Nominal return from capital, construction	(457)
Nominal return from capital, transport	(458)
Nominal return from capital, other	(459)
Changes in the rates of return on capital	(485)
Labor productivity changes	
Labor productivity changes in mineral	(462)
Labor productivity changes in other	(466)
Capital productivity changes	
Capital productivity changes for all sectors	(433, 467–473)
Demography	
Dependency ratio	(623)
Working population	(695)
Output	
Growth area under irrigated rice	(509)

	Variable number
Growth area under nonirrigated rice	(514)
Growth, fertilizer	(510)
Growth area under other agriculture	(516)
Growth area under tree crops	(519)
Growth value added, mineral	(247)
Growth value added, forestry	(205)
Growth value added, dwelling	(266)
GDP oil	(311)

Appendix B

Parameters

Agriculture

Elasticity of rice output changes to changes in irrigated area	1.8
Elasticity of rice output changes to changes in nonirrigated area	0.66
Elasticity of rice output changes to changes in fertilizer use	0.59
Elasticity of tree crop output changes to changes in area	0.998
Elasticity of other agriculture output changes to changes in area	0.51
Elasticity of other agriculture output changes to changes in land productivity	0.089
Elasticity of vegetable output changes to changes in vegetable demand	1.0
Ratio of value added to output, fishing	0.90
Ratio of value added to output, animal husbandry	0.90
Ratio of value added to output, rice	0.96
Ratio of value added to output, tree crops	0.40
Ratio of value added to output, forestry	0.89
ICOR, animal	2.23
ICOR, fishing	2.88
ICOR, forestry	0.57
ICOR, tree crops	8.20
ICOR, other agriculture	2.00
Increase in intermediate imports of animal husbandry	3 percent

Domestic demand elasticity for tree crops to changes in constant GDP at factor costs	0.60
Domestic consumption parameter of forestry	8 percent
Employment elasticity, agriculture	0.20
Fish: expenditure elasticity, class 1	1.75
Fish: expenditure elasticity, class 2	1.44
Fish: expenditure elasticity, class 3	1.13
Fish: expenditure elasticity, class 4	0.725
Animal husbandry: expenditure elasticity, class 1	3.00
Animal husbandry: expenditure elasticity, class 2	2.38
Animal husbandry: expenditure elasticity, class 3	1.86
Animal husbandry: expenditure elasticity, class 4	1.29
Vegetables: expenditure elasticity, class 1	1.04
Vegetables: expenditure elasticity, class 2	1.06
Vegetables: expenditure elasticity, class 3	1.11
Vegetables: expenditure elasticity, class 4	1.12
Rice: expenditure elasticity, class 1	1.81
Rice: expenditure elasticity, class 2	0.717
Rice: expenditure elasticity, class 3	0.447
Rice: expenditure elasticity, class 4	−0.14
Nonagriculture	
Ratio of value added to output, consumption goods	0.50
Ratio of value added to output, capital goods	0.25
Ratio of value added to output, public work	0.40
Ratio of value added to output, construction	0.40
Ratio of value added to output, mineral	0.50
Ratio of value added to output, electricity	0.70
ICOR, capital goods (3-year lag)	4.0
ICOR, intermediate goods (3-year lag)	4.0
ICOR, consumption goods, capital intensive (3-year lag)	2.7
ICOR, consumption goods, labor intensive (2-year lag)	2.5
ICOR, small-scale manufacturing (1-year lag)	1.5
ICOR, transport (3-year lag)	6.0
ICOR, banking (1-year lag)	1.2
ICOR, services (1-year lag)	1.2
ICOR, trade (1-year lag)	1.0
ICOR, public administration (1-year lag)	1.2
ICOR, construction and dwelling (1-year lag)	2.0
ICOR, electricity (1-year lag)	10.0
Demand elasticity for trade in the goods sector	1.10

Demand elasticity for transport in the goods sector	1.10
Demand elasticity for banking in the goods sector	1.10
Demand elasticity for services in the goods sector	1.00
Employment elasticity, large-scale manufacturing	0.35
Employment elasticity, small-scale manufacturing	0.6
Employment elasticity, construction	0.6
Employment elasticity, electricity	0.2
Employment elasticity, transport	0.4
Employment elasticity, banking	0.6
Employment elasticity, services	0.5
Employment elasticity, trade	0.5
Employment elasticity, public administration	0.5
Percent of working population in mineral	2 percent
Percent of public administration to GNP	16.8 percent
Income per capita, public works (rupiahs)	40,000
Mineral component of large-scale manufacturing	2.1 percent
Construction component of capital formation:	
Mining, manufacturing, and transport	30 percent
Rest of the economy excluding rural development	65 percent
Machinery component of capital formation	45 percent
Industry electricity demand coefficient per unit output:	
Capital goods	0.45
Intermediate goods	0.196
Consumption goods, capital intensive	0.035
Consumption goods, labor intensive	0.082
Consumer electricity demand as a percentage of GDP	14 percent
Base period investment allocation between:	
Capital goods	7.7 percent
Intermediate goods	55.2 percent
Consumption goods, capital intensive	12.6 percent
Consumption goods, labor intensive	24.5 percent
Working capital as a percentage of GDP changes	20 percent
Replacement capital as a percentage of GDP	1 percent
Demand elasticity for manufactured consumption goods:	
Lower-income classes	1.0
Higher-income classes	1.3
Intermediate import-output elasticity	1.008
Price elasticity for intermediate imports	2.78

Public finance

Direct tax elasticity to changes in current GDP	1.3

Indirect tax elasticity to changes in current GDP	1.13
Import tax elasticity to changes in imports	1.166
Export tax elasticity to changes in exports	1.098
Income and expenditure	
Real savings interest	7 percent
Minimum disposable income before savings (rupiahs)	40,000
Income per capita, unemployed labor	1,000
1973 average disposable income, income class 1	16,600
Efficiency elasticity to standard of living	0.15
Minimum income requirement (rupiahs)	24,000
Income elasticity, lower-income classes	0.8
Income elasticity, higher-income classes	0.3
Domestic component of gross domestic expenditure	88 percent
Imported component of gross domestic expenditure	12 percent
Phillips curve wage cutoff point	5 percent
Wage adjustment	2 percent
Monetary	
Demand elasticity for money to:	
Changes in real output	0.529
Changes in last year's real money balances	0.729
Inflation rates	−0.518

Appendix C

Explanation of Variables in the Model

THE VARIABLES ARE identified here in numerical order, first for the debt submodel and then for the main model. For the equation system, see Appendix D.

Debt Submodel

Number	*Variable*
11	Amortization, new loans, other development assistance
14	Amortization, new loans, multilateral agencies
15	Amortization, new loans, commercial credits
16	Amortization, new loans, Export-Import Bank
18	Amortization, new loans, private governments
20	Amortization, new loans, other governments
21	Interest, new loans, other development assistance
24	Interest, new loans, multilateral agencies
25	Interest, new loans, commercial credits
26	Interest, new loans, Export-Import Bank
28	Interest, new loans, private governments
30	Interest, new loans, other governments
36	New commitments, other development assistance
40	New commitments, multilateral agencies
45	New commitments, commercial credits
46	New commitments, Export-Import Bank
48	New commitments, private governments
50	New commitments, other governments
60	New commitments, grants

Number	*Variable*
73	New disbursements, other development assistance
77	New disbursements, multilateral agencies
82	New disbursements, commercial credits
83	New disbursements, Export-Import Bank
85	New disbursements, private governments
86	Net private transfers
87	New disbursements, other governments
97	New disbursements, grants
107	Total new commitments
122	Total new disbursements
127	Total amortization, new loans
128	New net disbursements, other development assistance
132	New net disbursements, multilateral agencies
133	New net disbursements, commercial credits
134	New net disbursements, Export-Import Bank
135	New net disbursements, private governments
136	New net disbursements, other governments
137	New net disbursements, total
142	Total interest, new loans
143	New net transfers, other development assistance
147	New net transfers, multilateral agencies
148	New net transfers, commercial credits
149	New net transfers, Export-Import Bank
150	New net transfers, private governments
151	New net transfers, other governments
152	New net transfers, total
158	Debt outstanding and disbursed, other development assistance
162	Debt outstanding and disbursed, multilateral agencies
163	Debt outstanding and disbursed, commercial credits
164	Debt outstanding and disbursed, Export-Import Bank
165	Debt outstanding and disbursed, private governments
166	Debt outstanding and disbursed, other governments
167	Debt outstanding and disbursed, total
168	Debt outstanding and disbursed, grants
169	Total existing disbursements
170	Total existing amortization
171	Total existing interest
172	Total existing net disbursements
173	Total existing net transfers

Number	*Variable*
174	Total existing debt outstanding
175	Total existing commitments
176	Total disbursements
177	Total amortization
178	Total interest
179	Total net disbursements
180	Total net transfers
181	Total debt outstanding and disbursed
182	Total commitments
197	Ratio of total interest to total debt outstanding
198	Ratio of total amortization to total debt outstanding
199	Ratio of total debt service to total debt outstanding
303	Foreign savings
421	Net transfers

Main Model

71	Export price index
72	Import price index
154	Terms of trade index
156	Terms of trade adjustment
157	Exports adjusted for terms of trade
192	Current factor service income
195	Time
200	Select variable
201	Total expenditure, fishery
202	Total expenditure, animal husbandry
203	Value added, tree crops
204	Value added, other agriculture
205	Value added, forestry
206	Value added, fishing
207	Average expenditure, income class 1, fishery
208	Average expenditure, income class 2, fishery
209	Average expenditure, income class 3, fishery
210	Average expenditure, income class 4, fishery
211	Average expenditure, income class 1, animal husbandry
214	Average expenditure, income class 2, animal husbandry
215	Gross national product, current market price
216	Average expenditure, income class 3, animal husbandry
217	Average expenditure, income class 4, animal husbandry
218	Average expenditure, income class 1, vegetables

Number	*Variable*
219	Average expenditure, income class 2, vegetables
220	Average expenditure, income class 3, vegetables
221	Average expenditure, income class 4, vegetables
222	Total expenditure, vegetables
223	Average expenditure, income class 1, rice
224	Average expenditure, income class 2, rice
225	Average expenditure, income class 3, rice
226	Average expenditure, income class 4, rice
227	Total expenditure, rice
228	Labor productivity, service sector
229	Income per capita, service
230	Labor productivity, trade
231	Income per capita, trade
232	Value added, goods sector
233	Labor, public works
234	Value added, agriculture
235	Value added, large-scale manufacturing
236	Labor, mineral
237	Constant price exports, tree crops
238	Constant price exports, forestry
239	Constant price exports, animal husbandry and fishing
240	Value added, rice
241	Value added, manufacturing
242	Investment, manufacturing
243	Population, public works
244	Population, mineral
245	Population, labor surplus absorption
246	Saving at constant prices
247	Value added, mineral
248	Value added, construction
249	Constant price demand, consumer goods
250	Value added, trade
251	Value added, transport
252	Value added, banking
253	Value added, public administration
254	Value added, electricity
255	Value added, dwelling
256	Nonwage index change, hard mineral and oil
257	Average propensity to save, income class 2
258	Average propensity to save, income class 3

Number	*Variable*
259	Average propensity to save, income class 4
260	Current price, nontax revenue
261	Growth transport sector
262	Constant price demand for consumer goods, low-income group
263	Constant price demand for consumer goods, high-income group
264	Export price, non-oil
265	Export price, oil
266	Growth rate, dwelling
267	Income, labor absorption sector
268	GDP, factor cost (non-oil)
269	Constant exports, non-oil sector
270	Current exports, oil
271	Constant exports, hard mineral
272	Value added, public work
273	Constant exports, oil
274	Terms of trade index, non-oil sector
275	Terms of trade index, oil sector
277	Real wage index
278	Abnormal profit rate
279	Intended investment total
280	Total investment
281	Investment, oil
282	Investment, mineral
283	Investment, construction
284	Investment, trade
285	Investment, banking
286	Investment, electricity
287	Net investment
288	Working capital
289	GDP current factor cost
290	Ratio of external capital inflow to GDP
291	Terms of trade adjustment, oil sector
292	Constant direct taxes
293	Current direct taxes
294	Current indirect taxes
295	Current import taxes
296	Current export taxes
297	GDP deflator

Number	*Variable*
298	Current imports
299	Current exports
300	Exchange rates
301	Domestic savings current price
302	Constant price subsidies
303	Foreign savings
304	Cost of living index
305	Total savings current
306	Total investment
307	Adjusted wage index
308	Export, non-oil sector, or capacity to import
309	Investment, agriculture
310	Export oil sector, or capacity to import
311	GDP oil sector
312	Investment, rural development
313	Gross domestic income, non-oil sector
314	Gross domestic income, oil sector
315	Current imports, intermediate goods
316	Current imports, capital goods
317	Current imports, consumer goods
318	Constant indirect taxes
319	Constant nontaxes
320	Government current revenues
321	Current oil revenue
322	Constant government expenditure
323	Value added, vegetables
324	Value added, animal husbandry
325	Gross domestic income
326	Investment, transport
327	Household savings
328	Total resources gap
329	Gross national income, non-oil sector
330	Gross national income, oil sector
331	Gross national income
332	Domestic price index, food
333	Domestic price index, other agriculture
334	Domestic price index, manufacturing
335	Domestic price index, construction
336	Domestic price index, transport
337	Domestic price index, other domestic

Number	*Variable*
338	Value-added coefficient, food
339	Value-added coefficient, other agriculture
340	Value-added coefficient, mineral
341	Value-added coefficient, manufacturing
342	Value-added coefficient, construction
343	Value-added coefficient, transport
344	Value-added coefficient, other
345	Tariff change, dummy 1
346	Exchange rate change, dummy 2
347	Subsidies, income class 1
348	Subsidies, income class 2
349	Subsidies, income class 3
350	Constant exports
351	Constant price, imports, intermediate goods
352	Constant price, imports, capital goods
353	Constant price, imports, consumer goods
354	Total resources availability (gross domestic income* plus resource gap)
355	GNP, non-oil sector
356	GNP, oil sector
357	Import substitution of intermediate imports
359	Constant price, imports, rice
360	Constant price, imports, total
361	Current total gap
362	Constant exports, oil sector
363	Current exports, tree crops
364	Current exports, forestry
365	Current exports, animal husbandry and fishing
366	Current exports, hard mineral
367	Current exports, manufacturing
368	Constant import, nonfactor services
369	Current imports, rice
370	Exchange rate change index
371	Constant imports, intermediate goods adjusted
372	Adjusted import price index
373	Constant imports adjusted
374	Current imports, intermediate goods adjusted
375	GNP total

* Gross domestic income is GDP adjusted for changes in terms of trade.

Number	*Variable*
376	Consumption, total
377	Domestic saving
378	Disposable income, total
379	Population total
380	Replacement capital
381	Relative population, income class 1
382	Relative population, income class 2
383	Relative population, income class 3
384	Relative population, income class 4
385	Relative disposable income, class 1
386	Relative disposable income, class 2
387	Relative disposable income, class 3
388	Relative disposable income, class 4
389	Cumulative relative disposable income, class 1
390	Cumulative relative disposable income, class 2
391	Cumulative relative disposable income, class 3
392	Cumulative relative disposable income, class 4
393	Gini coefficient
394	National saving
395	Reserve money
396	Money
397	ICOR, capital goods
398	ICOR, intermediate goods
399	ICOR, consumer goods, capital intensive
400	ICOR, consumer goods, labor intensive
401	ICOR, animal husbandry
402	ICOR, fishing
403	ICOR, tree crops
404	ICOR, other agriculture
405	Current subsidies
406	ICOR, construction
407	ICOR, trade
408	ICOR, banking
409	ICOR, electricity
410	Unemployment rate
412	Total expenditure last year
414	Current imports, adjusted
415	Current total gap, adjusted
416	ICOR, transport
417	ICOR, services

Number	*Variable*
418	ICOR, public administration
419	ICOR, traditional industries
420	Minimum ICOR
421	Net transfers
425	Residual investment
426	Total imports (unadjusted) at current price, less rice and nonfactor services
427	Import of capital goods (switching technique to exports)
428	Import of consumption goods (switching technique to exports)
429	Import substitution ratio
430	Lagged constant price, capital goods imports
431	Lagged constant price, consumption goods imports
432	Lagged capital goods imports at current price
433	Capital productivity index
434	Current government expenditure
435	Export price index, manufacturing
436	Export price index, manufacturing, domestic
437	Export price index, tree crops, domestic
438	Export price index, forestry, domestic
439	Export price index, fishing and animal husbandry, domestic
440	Export price index, oil, domestic
441	Export price index, hard mineral
442	Lagged consumption goods imports at current price
443	Wage (labor income) index, food
444	Wage (labor income) index, other agriculture
445	Wage (labor income) index, mineral
446	Wage (labor income) index, manufacturing
447	Wage (labor income) index, construction
448	Wage (labor income) index, transport
449	Wage (labor income) index, other sectors
450	Total GDP, factor cost
451	Gross domestic income, factor cost
452	Consumption
453	Nonwage index, food
454	Nonwage index, other agriculture
455	Nonwage index, mineral
456	Nonwage index, change manufacturing
457	Nonwage index, change construction

Number	*Variable*
458	Nonwage index, change transport
459	Nonwage index, other
460	Labor productivity index, food
461	Labor productivity index, other agriculture
462	Labor productivity index, mineral
463	Labor productivity index, manufacturing
464	Labor productivity index, construction
465	Labor productivity index, transport
466	Labor productivity index, other
467	Capital productivity index, food
468	Capital productivity index, other agriculture
469	Capital productivity index, mineral
470	Capital productivity index, manufacturing
471	Capital productivity index, construction
472	Capital productivity index, transport
473	Capital productivity index, other
474	Import price index, food
475	Import price index, other agriculture
476	Import price index, mineral
477	Import price index, manufacturing
478	Import price index, construction
479	Import price index, transport
480	Import price index, other
481	Wage index change, food
482	Accumulated unemployment rate
483	Nonwage index change, other agriculture
484	Domestic savings
485	Nonwage index change
486	Price index, mineral
487	Consumption, domestic, at current price
488	Resource gap
489	Resource use
490	Money demand
491	Import price index, manufacturing
492	Import price index, food
493	Export price index, tree crops
494	Exchange rate index
495	Export price index, forestry
496	Export price index, fishing and animal husbandry
497	Export price index, oil

Number	*Variable*
498	Export price index, hard mineral
499	National saving
500	Current imports, nonfactor services
501	Accumulated surplus absorption
502	Domestic demand, tree crops
503	Investment, animal husbandry
504	Investment, fishing
505	Investment, forestry
506	Investment, tree crops
507	Investment, rice
508	Investment, other agriculture
509	Growth of area under irrigated rice
510	Growth of fertilizer use
511	Value added, rice, irrigated
512	Value added, rice, nonirrigated
513	Area under irrigated rice
514	Area under nonirrigated rice
515	Area under tree crops
516	Area under other agriculture
517	Fertilizer
518	Time trend
519	Growth of area under tree crops
520	Money transfers needed to reach minimum standard
521	Poverty index
522	Terms of trade, rural sector
523	Current discretionary taxes
524	Current expenditure economy
525	Nonfactor service income
526	GNP
527	Gross national income * constant
528	Cumulative savings, income class 1
529	Cumulative savings, income class 2
530	Percentage unemployed
531	Cumulative savings, income class 3
532	Labor surplus absorption
533	Population, trade sector
534	Constant exports, manufacturing
535	Government savings

* Gross national income is GNP adjusted for changes in terms of trade.

Number	*Variable*
536	Concessionary savings
537	Investment, services
538	Value added, services
539	Investment, public administration
540	Value added, capital goods
541	Investment, capital goods
542	Value added, intermediate goods
543	Investment, intermediate goods
544	Value added, consumption goods, capital intensive
545	Value added, consumption goods, labor intensive
546	Value added, traditional manufacturing
547	Investment consumption goods, labor intensive
548	Investment consumption goods, capital intensive
549	Investment, traditional industries
550	Expenditures, income class 1
551	Expenditures, income class 2
552	Expenditures, income class 3
553	Expenditures, income class 4
554	Total expenditures
555	Disposable income, class 1
556	Income, class 1
557	Indirect taxes, class 1
558	Disposable income, class 2
559	Income, class 2
560	Indirect taxes, income class 2
561	Disposable income, class 3
562	Income, class 3
563	Indirect taxes, income class 3
564	Disposable income, class 4
565	Income, class 4
566	Indirect taxes, income class 4
567	Average disposable income, class 1
568	Average disposable income, class 2
569	Average disposable income, class 3
570	Average disposable income, class 4
571	Population, income class 1
572	Population, income class 2
573	Population, income class 3
574	Population, income class 4
575	Population, agriculture, income class 1

Number	*Variable*
576	Population, large-scale manufacturing, income class 1
577	Population, small-scale manufacturing, income class 1
578	Population, construction, income class 1
579	Population, electricity, income class 1
580	Population, transport, income class 1
581	Population, banking, income class 1
582	Population, public administration, income class 1
583	Population, service, income class 1
584	Population, trade, income class 1
585	Population, agriculture, income class 2
586	Population, large-scale manufacturing, income class 2
587	Population, small-scale manufacturing, income class 2
588	Population, construction, income class 2
589	Population, electricity, income class 2
590	Population, transport, income class 2
591	Population, banking, income class 2
592	Population, public administration, income class 2
593	Population, service, income class 2
594	Population, trade, income class 2
595	Population, agriculture, income class 3
596	Population, large-scale manufacturing, income class 3
597	Population, small-scale manufacturing, income class 3
598	Population, construction, income class 3
599	Population, electricity, income class 3
600	Population, transport, income class 3
601	Population, banking, income class 3
602	Population, public administration, income class 3
603	Population, service, income class 3
604	Population, trade, income class 3
605	Population, agriculture, income class 4
606	Population, large-scale manufacturing, income class 4
607	Population, small-scale manufacturing, income class 4
608	Population, construction, income class 4
609	Population, electricity, income class 4
610	Population, transport, income class 4
611	Population, banking, income class 4
612	Population, public administration, income class 4
613	Population, service, income class 4
614	Population, trade, income class 4
615	Average expenditure, income class 1

Number	*Variable*
616	Average expenditure, income class 2
617	Average expenditure, income class 3
618	Average expenditure, income class 4
619	Average propensity to save, income class 1
620	Labor productivity, agriculture
621	Employment elasticity, agriculture
622	Income per capita, agriculture
623	Dependency ratio
624	Population, agriculture
625	Average income, class 1, agriculture
626	Average income, class 2, agriculture
627	Average income, class 3, agriculture
628	Average income, class 4, agriculture
629	Average income, class 1, large-scale manufacturing
630	Average income, class 2, large-scale manufacturing
631	Average income, class 3, large-scale manufacturing
632	Average income, class 4, large-scale manufacturing
633	Average income, class 1, small-scale manufacturing
634	Average income, class 2, small-scale manufacturing
635	Average income, class 3, small-scale manufacturing
636	Average income, class 4, small-scale manufacturing
637	Average income, class 1, construction
638	Average income, class 2, construction
639	Average income, class 3, construction
640	Average income, class 4, construction
641	Average income, class 1, electricity
642	Average income, class 2, electricity
643	Average income, class 3, electricity
644	Average income, class 4, electricity
645	Average income, class 1, transport
646	Average income, class 2, transport
647	Average income, class 3, transport
648	Average income, class 4, transport
649	Average income, class 1, banking
650	Average income, class 2, banking
651	Average income, class 3, banking
652	Average income, class 4, banking
653	Average income, class 1, public administration
654	Average income, class 2, public administration
655	Average income, class 3, public administration

Number	*Variable*
656	Average income, class 4, public administration
657	Average income, class 1, service
658	Average income, class 2, service
659	Average income, class 3, service
660	Average income, class 4, service
661	Average income, class 1, trade
662	Average income, class 2, trade
663	Average income, class 3, trade
664	Average income, class 4, trade
665	Labor productivity, large-scale manufacturing
666	Employment elasticity, large-scale manufacturing
667	Income per capita, large-scale manufacturing
668	Population, large-scale manufacturing
669	Labor productivity, small-scale manufacturing
670	Employment elasticity, small-scale manufacturing
671	Income per capita, small-scale manufacturing
672	Population, small-scale manufacturing
673	Labor productivity, construction
674	Employment elasticity, construction
675	Income per capita, construction
676	Population, construction
677	Labor productivity, electricity
678	Employment elasticity, electricity
679	Income per capita, electricity
680	Population, electricity
681	Labor productivity, transport
682	Employment elasticity, transport
683	Income per capita, transport
684	Population, transport
685	Labor productivity, banking
686	Employment elasticity, banking
687	Income per capita, banking
688	Population, banking
689	Labor productivity, public administration
690	Employment elasticity, public administration
691	Income per capita, public administration
692	Population, public administration
693	Employment elasticity, service
694	Surplus labor

Number	*Variable*
695	Labor force
696	Employment elasticity, trade
698	Value added, mineral
699	Total demand, intermediate goods
700	Population, service

Appendix D

The Equation System of the Model

THIS APPENDIX GIVES the equations in blocks, in terms of the variables. They are presented in Fortran computer language.

Y-values refer to endogenous variable numbers. *X*-values refer to exogenous variable numbers. Z-values refer to lagged endogenous variables: for example, Z(13,2) means the value of *Y*(13) of two years ago; "*" means multiplication; and "&" means addition.

"EXP" means anti-log and "A-log" means log of the variable. "If" statements give equation conditions.

The distribution mechanism in the model has two blocks: with the assumption that the average income of all income classes would grow by the same rate in which the output per labor would grow; and with an explicit specification of the labor market determining wage rates (block 100).

The ordering of the equations is important in the sense that it would help in a quicker convergence. But the present program can solve any nonlinear simultaneous system provided it shows recursivity intertemporally and is well behaved.

Debt Block

New public loan commitments

```
Y(36)=X(36)
  If(X[36].LT.1.)Y(36)=Z(36,1)*(1&X[36])
Y(38)=X(38)
  If(X[38].LT.1.)Y(38)=Z(38,1)*(1&X[38])
Y(40)=X(40)
  If(X[40].LT.1.)Y(40)=Z(40,1)*(1&X[40])
Y(46)=X(46)
  If(X[46].LT.1.)Y(46)=Z(46,1)*(1&X[46])
Y(107)=Y(36)&Y(38)&Y(40)&Y(46)
```

New public loan disbursement

```
Y(73)=X(73)
Y(75)=X(75)
Y(77)=X(77)
Y(83)=X(83)
```

Net transfer format

```
Y(113)=Y(1)+Y(73)
Y(114)=Y(2)+Y(74)
Y(115)=Y(3)+Y(75)+Y(76)
Y(116)=Y(113)+Y(114)+Y(115)
Y(117)=Y(4)+Y(77)+Y(78)+Y(79)&Y(88)&Y(89)&Y(90)&Y(91)
Y(118)=Y(5)+Y(80)+Y(81)+Y(82)
Y(119)=Y(6)+Y(7)+Y(83)+Y(84)
Y(120)=Y(8)+Y(9)+Y(85)+Y(86)
Y(121)=Y(10)+Y(87)
Y(122)=Y(116)+Y(117)+Y(118)+Y(119)+Y(120)+Y(121)
Y(123)=Y(33)+Y(95)&Y(96)&Y(97)
Y(124)=Y(11)+Y(12)+Y(13)
Y(125)=Y(16)+Y(17)
Y(126)=Y(18)+Y(19)
Y(127)=Y(14)+Y(15)+Y(20)+Y(124)+Y(125)+Y(126)
Y(128)=Y(11)+Y(113)
Y(129)=Y(12)+Y(114)
Y(130)=Y(13)+Y(115)
Y(131)=Y(116)+Y(124)
Y(132)=Y(14)+Y(117)
Y(133)=Y(15)+Y(118)
Y(134)=Y(119)+Y(125)
Y(135)=Y(120)+Y(126)
Y(136)=Y(20)+Y(121)
Y(137)=Y(122)+Y(127)
Y(138)=Y(34)+Y(123)
```

```
Y(139)=Y(21)+Y(22)+Y(23)
Y(140)=Y(26)+Y(27)·
Y(141)=Y(28)+Y(29)
Y(142)=Y(24)+Y(25)+Y(30)+Y(139)+Y(140)+Y(141)
Y(143)=Y(21)+Y(128)
Y(144)=Y(22)+Y(129)
Y(145)=Y(23)+Y(130)
Y(146)=Y(131)+Y(139)
Y(147)=Y(24)+Y(132)
Y(148)=Y(25)+Y(133)
Y(149)=Y(134)+Y(140)
Y(150)=Y(135)+Y(141)
Y(151)=Y(30)+Y(136)
Y(152)=Y(137)+Y(142)
Y(153)=Y(35)+Y(138)
```

Debt outstanding and disbursed

```
Y(158)=Z(158,1)+Y(128)
Y(159)=Z(159,1)+Y(129)
Y(160)=Z(160,1)+Y(130)
Y(161)=Y(158)+Y(159)+Y(160)
Y(162)=Z(162,1)+Y(132)
Y(163)=Z(163,1)+Y(133)
Y(164)=Z(164,1)+Y(134)
Y(165)=Z(165,1)+Y(135)
Y(166)=Z(166,1)+Y(136)
Y(167)=Y(161)+Y(162)+Y(163)+Y(164)+Y(165)+Y(166)
Y(168)=Z(168,1)+Y(138)
```

ICOR

```
Y(397)=Z(397,1)-Z(420,1)
  If(Z[532,1].LT.0.0)Z(420,1)=0
Y(398)=Z(398,1)-Z(420,1)
  If(Z[532,1].LT.0.0)Z(420,1)=0
Y(399)=Z(399,1)-Z(420,1)
  If(Z[532,1].LT.0.0)Z(420,1)=0
Y(400)=Z(400,1)-Z(420,1)
  If(Z[532,1].LT.0.0)Z(420,1)=0
Y(401)=Z(401,1)-Z(420,1)
Y(402)=Z(402,1)-Z(420,1)
Y(403)=Z(403,1)-Z(420,1)
Y(404)=Z(404,1)-Z(420,1)
Y(406)=Z(406,1)-Z(420,1)
  If(Z[532,1].LT.0.0)Z(420.1)=0
Y(407)=Z(407,1)-Z(420,1)
  If(Z[532,1].LT.0.0)Z(420,1)=0
```

```
Y(408)=Z(408,1)-Z(420,1)
  If(Z[532,1].LT.0.0)Z(420,1)=0
Y(409)=Z(409,1)-Z(420,1)
  If(Z[532,1].LT.0.0)Z(420,1)=0
Y(416)=Z(416,1)-Z(420.1)
  If(Z[532,1].LT.0.0)Z(420,1)=0
Y(417)=Z(417,1)-Z(420,1)
Y(419)=Z(419,1)-Z(420,1)
  If(Z[532,1].LT.0.0)Z(420,1)=0
Y(417)=Z(417,1)-Z(420,1)
Y(418)=Z(418,1)-Z(420,1)
  If(Z[532,1].LT.0.0)Z(420,1)=0
```

Price Block

```
Y(423)=X(423)
```

Labor productivity

```
Y(460)=([Y{620}/.098]-1.)
Y(461)=([Y{620}/.098]-1.)
Y(462)=0.059
Y(463)=([Y{665}/.631]-1.)
Y(464)=([Y{673}/.277]-1.)
Y(465)=([Y{681}/.248]-1.)
Y(466)=0.059
```

Profit rate

```
Y(279)=X(279)
Y(278)=X(278)
Y(485)=X(485)&Z(485,1)
Y(483)=(Y[493]-Z[493,1])/Z(493,1)&Y(485)
Y(256)=(Y[497]-Z[497,1])/Z(497,1)&Y(485)
Y(453)=X(453)
  If(ABS[Y{453}].LT.1)Y(453)=Z(453,1)*(1&X[453])
Y(454)=Z(454,1)*(1.&Y[483])
Y(455)=Z(455,1)*(1.&Y[256])
Y(456)=Y(453)
Y(457)=Y(453)
Y(458)=Y(453)
Y(459)=Y(453)
```

Capital productivity

```
Y(433)=Z(433,1)*1.10
Y(467)=Y(433)
Y(468)=Y(433)
Y(469)=Y(433)
Y(470)=Y(433)
Y(471)=Y(433)
```

```
Y(472)=Y(433)
Y(473)=Y(433)
```

Export prices (1973 dollar = 1.00)

```
Y(493)=X(493)
  If(ABS[Y{493}].LT..3)Y(493)=Z(493,1)*(1&X[493])
Y(495)=X(495)
  If(ABS[Y{495}].LT..3)Y(495)=Z(495,1)*(1&X[495])
Y(496)=X(496)
  If(ABS[Y{496}].LT..3)Y(496)=Z(496,1)*(1&X[496])
Y(497)=X(497)
  If(ABS[Y{497}].LT..5)Y(497)=Z(497,1)*(1&X[497])
Y(498)=X(498)
  If(ABS[Y{498}].LT..5)Y(498)=Z(498,1)*(1&X[498])
Y(435)=X(435)
  If(ABS[Y{435}].LT..5)Y(435)=Z(435,1)*(1&X[435])
Y(187)=X(187)
  If(X[187].LT..5)Y(187)=Z(187,1)*(1&X[187])
Y(193)=X(193)
  If(X[193].LT..5)Y(193)=Z(193,1)*(1&X[193])
```

Export prices (1973 rupiah = 1.00)

```
Y(436)=Z(494,1)*Y(435)
Y(437)=Z(494,1)*Y(493)
Y(441)=Z(494,1)*Y(498)
Y(440)=Z(494,1)*Y(497)
Y(439)=Z(494,1)*Y(496)
Y(438)=Z(494,1)*Y(495)
Y(188)=Z(494,1)*Y(187)
Y(194)=Z(494,1)*Y(193)
```

Import prices

```
Y(492)-X(492)
Y(491)=X(491)
Y(474)=Z(494,1)*Y(492)
Y(475)=X(475)*Z(494,1)
Y(477)=Z(494,1)*X(477)
Y(476)=X(476)*Z(494,1)
Y(478)=Y(474)
Y(479)=X(479)*Z(494,1)
Y(480)=X(480)*Z(494,1)
```

Wage rate

```
Y(482)=Z(410,1)-.05
Y(481)=(Y[304]-Z[304,1])/Z(304,1)-Y(482)
Y(443)=Z(443,1)*(1.&Y[481])
Y(444)-Y(443)
```

```
Y(445)=Y(443)
Y(446)=Y(443)
Y(447)=Y(443)
Y(448)=Y(443)
Y(449)=Y(443)
```

Input-output matrix

```
Y(338)=0.041*(Y[443]-Y[460])&0.879*(Y[453]&Y[467])&0.010*Y(474)
Y(339)=0.145*(Y[444]-Y[461])&0.646*(Y[454]&Y[468])&0.007*Y(475)
Y(340)=0.221*(Y[445]-Y[462])&0.604*(Y[455]&Y[469])&0.004*Y(476)
Y(341)=0.079*(Y[446]-Y[463])&0.124*(Y[456]&Y[470])&0.085*Y(477)
Y(342)=0.267*(Y[447]-Y[464])&0.175*(Y[457]&Y[471])&0.045*Y(478)
Y(343)=0.237*(Y[448]-Y[465])&0.167*(Y[458]&Y[472])&0.005*Y(479)
Y(344)=0.288*(Y[449]-Y[466])&0.441*(Y[459]&Y[473])&0.000*Y(480)
```

Price matrix

```
Y(332)=([1.025*Y{338}&0.003*Y{339}&0.000*Y{340}&0.010*Y{341}&
        0.000*Y{342}&0.033*Y{343}&0.063*Y{344}]*1.2)*(1.&Y[278])
  If(X[332].NE..0)Y(332)=X(332)
Y(333)=(.039*Y[338]&1.089*Y[339]&0.004*Y[340]&0.085*Y[341]&
        0.000*Y[342]&0.016*Y[343]&0.099*Y[344])*(1.&Y[278])
  If(X[333].NE..0)Y(333)=X(333)
Y(486)=(.018*Y[338]&0.010*Y[339]&1.042*Y[340]&0.050*Y[341]&
        0.004*Y[342]&0.008*Y[343]&0.144*Y[344])*(1.&Y[278])
  If(X[486].NE..0)Y(486)=X(486)
Y(334)=(.359*Y[338]&0.179*Y[339]&0.046*Y[340]&1.121*Y[341]&
        0.001*Y[342]&0.023*Y[343]&0.246*Y[344])*(1.&Y[278])
  If(X[334].NE..0)Y(334)=X(334)
Y(335)=(.067*Y[338]&0.147*Y[339]&0.149*Y[340]&0.205*Y[341]&
        1.005*Y[342]&0.042*Y[343]&0.307*Y[344])*(1.&Y[278])
  If(X[335].NE..0)Y(335)=X(335)
Y(336)=(.088*Y[338]&0.045*Y[339]&0.011*Y[340]&0.273*Y[341]&
        0.002*Y[342]&1.098*Y[343]&0.354*Y[344])*(1.&Y[278])
  If(X[336].NE..0)Y(336)=X(336)
Y(337)=(.036*Y[338]&0.019*Y[339]&0.005*Y[340]&0.099*Y[341]&
        0.004*Y[342]&0.046*Y[343]&1.466*Y[344])*(1.&Y[278])
  If(X[337].NE..0)Y(337)=X(337)
Y(297)=.167*Y(332)&.122*Y(333)&.042*Y(486)&.265*Y(334)&.036*
        Y(335)&.056*Y(336)&.311*Y(337)
Y(304)=.88*Y(297)&.12*Y(477)
Y(522)=Y(332)/Y(304)
```

Surplus Labor Block

```
Y(532)=Z(532,1)&Y(501)
Y(623)=X(623)*1.36
Y(267)=([Y{532}*Y{623}]/[1.0E&6]*1000.
Y(410)=(Z(694,1)&Z(532,1))/Z(695,1)
```

```
Y(307)=X(307)
Y(277)= 1.&[.4*([Z{268,1}-Z{268,2}]/Z{268,1})]
```

Output Block (Value Added, 1973 Constant)

```
Y(312)=X(312)
Y(509)=1.02
  If(Y[195].GT.1985.)
Y(509)=1.016
Y(510)=X(510)
Y(513)=Z(513,1)*Y(509)
Y(517)=Z(517,1)*Y(510)
Y(511)=Z(511,1)*1.004*(1.&1.87*[Y{513}-Z{513,1}]/Z[513,1]&
        .059*[Y{517}-{517,1}]/Z[517,1])
Y(514)=Z(514,1)*1.005
Y(512)=Z(512,1)*1.00*(1.&.66*[Y{514}-Z{514,1}]/Z[514,1])
  If(Y[195].GE.1976.)
Y(512)=Z(512,1)*1.00*(1.&.70*[Y{514}-Z{514,1}]/Z[514,1])
    If(Y[195].GT.1980.)
Y(512)=Z(512,1)*1.00*(1.&.85*[Y{514}-Z{514,1}]/Z[514,1])
    If(Y[195].GT.1985.)
Y(512)=Z(512,1)*1.00*(1.&1.0*[Y{514}-Z{514,1}]/Z[514,1])
Y(240)=Y(511)&Y(512)
Y(519)=X(519)
  If(Y[195].GT.1990.)Y(519)=1.014
Y(515)=Z(515,1)*Y(519)
Y(203)=Z(203,1)*(1.&1.25*[Y{515}-Z{515,1}]/Z[515,1])
  If(Y[195].GT.1980.)
Y(203)=Z(203,1)*(1.&1.75*[Y{515}-Z{515,1}]/Z[515,1])
  If(Y[195].GT.1990.)
Y(203)=Z(203,1)*(1.&2.50*[Y{515}-Z{515,1}]/Z[515,1])
Y(516)=Z(516,1)*1.05
  If(Y[195].GT.1985.)Y(516)=Z(516,1)*1.04
  If(Y[195].GT.1990.)Y(516)=Z(516,1)*1.03
Y(518)=Z(518,1)&1.
Y(204)=Z(204,1)*(1.&.51*[Y{516}-Z{516,1}]/Z[516,1]
        &.089*[Y{518}-Z{518,1}]/Z[518,1])
  If(Y[195].GE.1976)
Y(204)=Z(204,1)*(1.&.60*[Y{516}-Z{516,1}]/Z[516,1]
        &.089*[Y{518}-Z{518,1}]/Z[518,1])
  If(Y[195].GT.1985)
Y(204)=Z(204,1)*(1.&.87*[Y{516}-Z{516,1}]/Z[516,1]
        &.089*[Y{518}-Z{518,1}]/Z[518,1])
  If(Y[195].GT.1990.)
Y(204)=Z(204,1)*(1.&1.33*[Y{516}-Z{516,1}]/Z[516,1]
        &.080*[Y{518}-Z{518,1}]/Z[518,1])
Y(205)=Z(205,1)*1.07
```

```
Y(239)=X(239)
  If(ABS[Y{239}].LT.1)Y(239)=Z(239,1)*(1&X[239])
Y(206)=(Z[206,1]-Z[239,1]*.9*.93)*(1.&[Y{201}-Z{201,1}]/Z[201,1])
        &Y(239)*.90*.93
  If(Y[206]/Z[206,1].GT.1.05)Y(206)=Z(206,1)*1.05
  If( Y[195].GT.1980.) Y(206)=Z(206,1)*1.07
  If(Y[195].GT.1985.)Y(206)=Z(206,1)*1.08
  If( Y[195].GT.1990.) Y(206)=Z(206,1)*1.085
Y(323)=Z(323,1)*(1.&[{Y(222)-Z(222,1)}/Z{222,1}])&Y(183)
  If(Y[323]/Z[323,1].LT.1.05)Y(323)=Z(323,1)*1.05
Y(324)=Z(324,1)*(1.&[Y{202}-Z{202,1}]/Z[202,1])&Y(239)*.90*
        -Z(324,1)*.03
  If(Y[324]/Z[324,1].GT.1.06)Y(324)=Z(324,1)*1.06
  If(Y[195].GT.1980.)Y(324)=Z(324,1)*1.07
  If(Y[195].GT.1990.)Y(324)=Z(324,1)*1.085
Y(234)=Y(240)&Y(203)&Y(204)&Y(205)&Y(206)&Y(323)&Y(324)
Y(247)=Z(247,1)*1.08
Y(248)=Z(248,1)*(Y[280]-Z[280,1])/Z(280,1)
  If(Y[248].LT.[Z{248,1}*1.15])Y(248)=Z(248,1)*1.15
Y(232)=Y(241)&Y(234)&Y(247)&Y(248)
Y(250)=Z(250,1)*(1.&1.10*[{Y(232)-Z(232,1)}/Z{232,1}])
Y(251)=Z(251,1)*(1.&1.10*[{Y(232)-Z(232,1)}/Z{232,1}])
Y(252)=Z(252,1)*(1.&1.10*[{Y(232)-Z(232,1)}/Z{232,1}])
Y(253)=-33.9&.168*(Y[232]&Y[251]&Y[252])
Y(272)=Y(312)*0.4
Y(254)=(Y[540]*.45&Y[542]*.196&Y[544]*.035&Y[545]*.082)*.70&
        .0014*Z(268,1)
Y(266)=Z(266,1)&X(266)
Y(255)=Z(255,1)*Y(266)
Y(538)=Z(538,1)*(1.&1.00*[{Y(232)-Z(232,1)}/Z{232,1}])
  If(Y[532].LT.0.0)Y(538)=Z(538,1)*(1.&[{(Z(700,1)=Z(700,2))
                                /Z(700,2)}*.5/Y{693}])
  If( Y[532].LT.0.0.AND. Y[538].GT.Z[538,1]) Y(538)=Z(538.1)
Y(540)=Z(540,1)&(Z[541,1]&Z[541,2]&Z[541,3])*.33/Y(397)
  If(Y[540].GT.[Z{540,1}*1.5])Y(540)=Z(540,1)*1.3
Y(542)=Z(542,1)&Z[543,1]&Z[543,2]&Z[543,3])*.33/Y(398)
  If( Y[542].GT.[Z{542,1}*1.3]) Y(542)=Z(542,1)*1.3
Y(544)=Z(544,1)&(Z[547,1]&Z[547,2]&Z[547,3])*.33/Y(399)
  If(Y[544].GT.[Z{544,1}*1.3])Y(544)=Z(544,1)*1.2
Y(545)=Z(545,1)&(Z[548,1]&Z[548,2])*.50/Y(400)
  If(Y[545].GT.[Z{545,1}*1.3])Y(545)=Z(545,1)*1.15
Y(235)=Y(540)&Y(542)&Y(544)&Y(545)
Y(546)=Z(546,1)*(1.&.8*[{Y(555)&Y(558)&Y(561)-Z(555,1)-Z(558,1)
        -Z(561,1)}/{Z(555,1)&Z(558,1)&Z(561,1)}]
          &.3*[{Y(564)-Z(564.1)}/Z{564,1}])&Y(189)
Y(241)=Y(540)&Y(542)&Y(544)&Y(545)&Y(546)
```

```
Y(268)=Y(232)&Y(255)&Y(250)&Y(251)&Y(252)&Y(253)&Y(254)
        &Y(538)&Y(267)&Y(272)
Y(289)=Y(268)*Y(297)
```

Export Block

Export 1973

```
Y(502)=Z(502,1)*(1.&.60*[{Y(268)-Z(268,1)}/Z{268,1}])
Y(237)=Y(203)*2.5-Y(502)
Y(238)=Y(205)*1.12-.008*Y(268)
Y(362)=X(362)*.415
Y(271)=Y(247)*2.0-Y(235)*.021
Y(534)=X(534)*.415
  If(ABS[Y{534}].LT.1)Y(534)=Z(534,1)*(1&X[534])
Y(183)=Z(183,1)*1.05
Y(184)=Z(184,1)*1.05
Y(189)=Z(189,1)*1.07
Y(350)=Y(237)&Y(238)&Y(239)&Y(362)&Y(271)&Y(534)
        -7(427,1)-Z(428,1)&Y(183)&Y(184)&Y(189)
```

Export current

```
Y(363)=Y(237)*Y(437)
Y(364)=Y(238)*Y(438)
Y(365)=Y(239)*Y(439)
Y(270)=Y(362)*Y(440)
Y(366)=Y(271)*Y(441)
Y(367)=Y(534)*Y(436)
Y(185)=Y(183)*Y(188)
Y(186)=Y(184)*Y(188)
Y(190)=Y(189)*Y(436)
Y(299)=Y(363)&Y(364)&Y(365)&Y(270)&Y(366)&Y(367)
        -Z(427,1)*Y(436)-Z(428,1)*Y(436)&Y(185)&Y(186)&Y(190)
```

Import Block

Import 1973

```
  If(Y[241].LE.0)Y(241)=100.
Y(351)=Z(351.1)*(1&1.008*[Y{241}/Z{241.1}-1.])
Y(352)=Y(280)*.45-Y(540)*4.
  If(Y[352].LT.0.0)Y(352)=0.0
Y(427)=Y(280)*.45-Y(540)*4.
  If(Y[427].GT.0.0)Y(427)=0.0
Y(368)=Y(500)/Y(480)
```

Import current

```
Y(500)=X(500)
  If(ABS[Y{500}].LT.1)Y(500)=Z(500,1)*(1&X[500])
```

```
Y(315)= Y(351)* Y(474)
Y(316)= Y(352)* Y(477)
```

Fiscal Block

```
Y(523)=Z(523,1)*1.15
Y(524)=Z(524,1)*1.15
Y(321)=X(321)
   If(ABS[Y{321}].LT.1) Y(321)=Z(321.1)*(1&X[321])
Y(294)=Z(294,1)*(1.&1.13*[Y{289}/Z{289,1}-1.])
Y(318)= Y(294)/ Y(297)
Y(293)=Z(293,1)*(1.&1.30*[Y{289}/Z{289,1}-1.])
Y(292)=(Y[293]/Y[297])
Y(295)=EXP (-2,885&1.166* ALOG[{Z(315,1)&Z(316,1)&Z(317,1)}])
   If(Y[299].LE.Y[270])Y(299)=Y(270)*1.1
Y(296)=EXP(-3.709&1.098*ALOG[{Y(299)-Y(270)}])
Y(319)=X(319)
   If(ABS[Y{319}].LT.1)Y(319)=Z(319,1)*(1&X[319])
Y(260)=Y(319)*Y(297)
Y(320)=Y(321)&Y(293)&Y(294)&Y(295)&Y(296)&Y(260)
Y(302)=X(302)
   If(ABS[Y{302}].LT.1)Y(302)=Z(302,1)*(1&X[302])
Y(405)=Y(302)*Y(297)
Y(322)=X(322)
   If(ABS[Y{322}].LT.1)Y(322)=Z(322,1)*(1&X[322])
Y(434)=Y(322)*Y(297)-Y(524)
```

Gross national product current

```
Y(192)=X(192)
   If(ABS[Y{192}].LT.1)Y(192)=Z(192,1)*(1&X[192])
Y(215)=Y(289)&Y(294)&Y(295)&Y(296)-Y(192)
```

Income Distribution Block

```
Y(200)=X(200)&Z(200,1)
   If(Y[200].EQ.1.)
```

Go to 100

```
Y(620)=Z(620,1)*(1.&[1.-Y{621}]*[{(234)-Z(234,1)}/Z{234,1}])
Y(621)=X(621)&Z(621,1)
Y(622)=(Y[620]/Y[623])*(Y[332]/Y[297])
Y(624)=(Y[234]*Y[332]/Y[297]/Y(622)
Y(625)=Z(625,1)*(Y[622]/Z[622,1])
Y(626)=Z(626,1)*(Y[622]/Z[622,1])
Y(627)=Z(627,1)*(Y[622]/Z[622,1])
Y(628)=Z(628,1)*(Y[622]/Z[622,1])
Y(575)=Z(575,1)*(Y[624]/Z[624,1])
```

Y(585)=Z(585,1)*(Y[624]/Z[624,1])
Y(595)=Z(595,1)*(Y[624]/Z[624,1])
Y(605)=Z(605,1)*(Y[624]/Z[624,1])
Y(665)=Z(665,1)*(1.&[1.−Y{666}]*[{Y(235)−Z(235,1)}/Z{235,1}])
Y(666)=X(666)&Z(666,1)
Y(667)=(Y[665]/Y[623])*(Y[334]/Y[297])
Y(668)=(Y[235]*Y[334]/Y[297])/Y(667)
Y(629)=Z(629,1)*(Y[667]/Z[667,1])
Y(630)=Z(630,1)*(Y[667]/Z[667,1])
Y(631)=Z(631,1)*(Y[667]/Z[667,1])
Y(632)=Z(632,1)*(Y[667]/Z[667,1])
Y(576)=Z(576,1)*(Y[668]/Z[668,1])
Y(586)=Z(586,1)*(Y[668]/Z[668,1])
Y(596)=Z(596,1)*(Y[668]/Z[668,1])
Y(606)=Z(606,1)*(Y[668]/Z[668,1])
Y(669)=Z(669,1)*(1.&[1.−Y{670}]*[{Y(546)−Z(546,1)}/Z{546,1}])
Y(670)=X(670)&Z(670,1)
Y(671)=(Y[669]/Y[623])*(Y[334]/Y[297])
Y(672)=(Y[546]*Y[334]/Y[297])/Y(671)
Y(633)=Z(633,1)*(Y[671]/Z[671,1])
Y(634)=Z(634,1)*(Y[671]/Z[671,1])
Y(635)=Z(635,1)*(Y[671]/Z[671,1])
Y(636)=Z(636,1)*(Y[671]/Z[671,1])
Y(577)=Z(577,1)*(Y[672]/Z[672,1])
Y(587)=Z(587,1)*(Y[672]/Z[672,1])
Y(597)=Z(597,1)*(Y[672]/Z[672,1])
Y(607)=Z(607,1)*(Y[672]/Z[672,1])
Y(673)=Z(673,1)*(1.&[1.−Y{674}]*[{Y(248)−Z(248,1)}/Z{248,1}])
Y(674)=X(674)&Z(674,1)
Y(675)=(Y[673]/Y[623])*(Y[335]/Y[297])
Y(676)=(Y[248]*Y[335]/Y[297])/Y(675)
Y(578)=Z(578,1)*(Y[676]/Z[676,1])
Y(588)=Z(588,1)*(Y[676]/Z[676,1])
Y(598)=Z(598,1)*(Y[676]/Z[676,1])
Y(608)=Z(608,1)*(Y[676]/Z[676,1])
Y(637)=Z(637,1)*(Y[675]/Z[675,1])
Y(638)=Z(638,1)*(Y[675]/Z[675,1])
Y(639)=Z(639,1)*(Y[675]/Z[675,1])
Y(640)=Z(640,1)*(Y[675]/Z[675,1])
Y(677)=Z(677,1)*(1.&[1.−Y{678}]*[{Y(254)−Z(254,1)}/Z{254,1}])
Y(678)=X(678)&Z(678,1)
Y(679)=(Y[677]/Y[623])*(Y[334]/Y[297])
Y(680)=(Y[254]*Y[334]/Y[297])/Y(679)
Y(579)=Z(579,1)*(Y[680]/Z[680,1])
Y(589)=Z(589,1)*(Y[680]/Z[680,1])
Y(599)=Z(599,1)*(Y[680]/Z[680,1])
Y(609)=Z(609,1)*(Y[680]/Z[680,1])

```
Y(641)=Z(641,1)*(Y[679]/Z[679,1])
Y(642)=Z(642,1)*(Y[679]/Z[679,1])
Y(643)=Z(643,1)*(Y[679]/Z[679,1])
Y(644)=Z(644,1)*(Y[679]/Z[679,1])
Y(681)=Z(681,1)*(1.&[1.-Y{682}]*[{(251)-Z(251,1)}/Z{252,1}])
Y(682)=X(682)&Z(682,1)
Y(683)=(Y[681]/Y[623])*(Y[336]/Y[297])
Y(684)=(Y[251]*Y[336]/Y[297])/Y(683)
Y(580)=Z(580,1)*(Y[684]/Z[684,1])
Y(590)=Z(590,1)*(Y[684]/Z[684,1])
Y(600)=Z(600,1)*(Y[684]/Z[684,1])
Y(610)=Z(610,1)*(Y[684]/Z[684,1])
Y(645)=Z(645,1)*(Y[683]/Z[683,1])
Y(646)=Z(646,1)*(Y[683]/Z[683,1])
Y(647)=Z(647,1)*(Y[683]/Z[683,1])
Y(648)=Z(648,1)*(Y[683]/Z[683,1])
Y(685)=Z(685,1)*(1.&[1.-Y{686}]*[{Y(252)-Z(252,1)}/Z{252,1}])
Y(686)=X(686)&Z(686,1)
Y(687)=(Y[685]/Y[623])*(Y[337]/Y[297])
Y(688)=(Y[252]*Y[337]/Y[297])/Y(687)
Y(581)=Z(581,1)*(Y[688]/Z[688,1])
Y(591)=Z(591,1)*(Y[688]/Z[688,1])
Y(601)=Z(601,1)*(Y[688]/Z[688,1])
Y(611)=Z(611,1)*(Y[688]/Z[688,1])
Y(649)=Z(649,1)*(Y[687]/Z[687,1])
Y(650)=Z(650,1)*(Y[687]/Z[687,1])
Y(651)=Z(651,1)*(Y[687]/Z[687,1])
Y(652)=Z(652,1)*(Y[687]/Z[687,1])
Y(689)=Z(689,1)*(1.&[1.-Y{690}]*[{Y(253)-Z(253,1)}/Z{253,1}])
Y(690)=X(690)&Z(690,1)
Y(691)=(Y[689]/Y[623])*(Y[337]/Y[297])
Y(692)=(Y[253]*Y[337]/Y[297])/Y(691)
Y(582)=Z(582,1)*(Y[692]/Z[692,1])
Y(592)=Z(592,1)*(Y[692]/Z[692,1])
Y(602)=Z(602,1)*(Y[692]/Z[692,1])
Y(612)=Z(612,1)*(Y[692]/Z[692,1])
Y(653)=Z(653,1)*(Y[691]/Z[691,1])
Y(654)=Z(654,1)*(Y[691]/Z[691,1])
Y(655)=Z(655,1)*(Y[691]/Z[691,1])
Y(656)=Z(656,1)*(Y[691]/Z[691,1])
Y(228)=Z(228,1)*(1.&[1.-Y{693}]*[{Y(538)-Z(538,1)}/Z{538,1}])
Y(693)=X(693)&Z(693,1)
Y(229)=(Y[228]/Y[623])*(Y[337]/Y[297])
Y(700)=(Y[538]*Y[337]/Y[297])/Y(229)
Y(583)=Z(583,1)*(Y[700]/Z[700,1])
```

```
Y(593)=Z(593,1)*(Y[700]/Z[700,1])
Y(603)=Z(603,1)*(Y[700]/Z[700,1])
Y(613)=Z(613,1)*(Y[700]/Z[700,1])
Y(657)=Z(657,1)*(Y[229]/Z[229,1])
Y(658)=Z(658,1)*(Y[229]/Z[229,1])
Y(659)=Z(659,1)*(Y[229]/Z[229,1])
Y(660)=Z(660,1)*(Y[229]/Z[229,1])
Y(230)=Z(230,1)*(1.&[1.-Y{696}]*[{Y(250)-Z(250,1)}/Z{250,1}])
Y(696)=X(696)&Z(696,1)
Y(231)=(Y[230]/Y[623])*(Y[337]/Y[297])
Y(533)=(Y[250]*Y[337]/Y[297])/Y(231)
Y(584)=Z(584,1)*(Y[533]/Z[533,1])
Y(594)=Z(594,1)*(Y[533]/Z[533,1])
Y(604)=Z(604,1)*(Y[533]/Z[533,1])
Y(614)=Z(614,1)*(Y[533]/Z[533,1])
Y(661)=Z(661,1)*(Y[231]/Z[231,1])
Y(662)=Z(662,1)*(Y[231]/Z[231,1])
Y(663)=Z(663,1)*(Y[231]/Z[231,1])
Y(664)=Z(664,1)*(Y[231]/Z[231,1])
```

Go to 200
100 continue

```
Y(620)=Z(620,1)*(1.&[1.-Y{621}]*[{Y(234)-Z(234,1)}/Z{234,1}])
Y(621)=X(621)&Z(621,1)
Y(622)=(Y[620]/Y[623])*(Y[332]/Y[297])
Y(624)=(Y[234]*Y[332]/Y[297])/Y(622)
Y(575)-Z(575,1)*(Y[624]/Z[624,1])
Y(585)=Z(585,1)*(Y[624]/Z[624,1])
Y(595)=Z(595,1)*(Y[624]/Z[624,1])
Y(605)=Z(605,1)*(Y[624]/Z[624,1])
Y(625)=Z(625,1)*Y(277)
Y(626)=Z(626,1)*Y(277)
Y(627)-Z(627,1)*(Y[622]/Z[622,1])
Y(628)=(Y[234]*Y[332]/Y[297]-Y[625]/[1.0E&6]*Y[575]-Y[626]/
        [1.0E&6]*Y[585]-Y[627]/[1.0E&6]*Y[595])/Y(605)*(1.0E&6)
Y(665)=Z(665,1)*(1.&[1.-Y{666}]*[{Y(235)-Z(235,1)}/Z{235,1}])
Y(666)=X(666)&Z(666,1)
Y(667)=(Y[665]/Y[623])*(Y[334]/Y[297])
Y(668)=(Y[235]*Y[334]/Y[297])/Y(667)
Y(576)=Z(576,1)*(Y[668]/Z[668,1])
Y(586)=Z(586,1)*(Y[668]/Z[668,1])
Y(596)=Z(596,1)*(Y[668]/Z[668,1])
Y(606)=Z(606,1)*(Y[668]/Z[668,1])
Y(629)=Z(629,1)*Y(277)
Y(630)=Z(630,1)*Y(277)
```

```
Y(631)=Z(631,1)*(Y[667]/Z[667,1])
Y(632)=(Y[235]*Y[334]/Y[297]-Y[629]/[1.0E&6]*Y[576]-Y[630]/
        [1.0E&6]*Y[586]-Y[631]/[1.0E&6]*Y[596])/Y(606)*(1.0E&6)
Y(669)=Z(669,1)*(1.&[1.-Y{670}]*[{Y(546)-Z(546,1)}/Z{546,1}])
Y(670)=X(670)&Z(670,1)
Y(671)=(Y[669]/Y[623])*(Y[334]/Y[297])
Y(672)=(Y[546]*Y[334]/Y[297])/Y(671)
Y(577)=Z(577,1)*(Y[672]/Z[672,1])
Y(587)=Z(587,1)*(Y[672]/Z[672,1])
Y(597)=Z(597,1)*(Y[672]/Z[672,1])
Y(607)=Z(607,1)*(Y[672]/Z[672,1])
Y(633)=Z(633,1)*Y(277)
Y(634)=Z(634,1)*Y(277)
Y(635)=Z(635,1)*(Y[671]/Z[671,1])
Y(636)=(Y[546]*Y[334]/Y[297]-Y[633]/[1.0E&6]*Y[577]-Y[634]/
        [1.0E&6]*Y[587]-Y[635]/[1.0E&6]*Y[597])/Y(607)*(1.0E&6)
Y(673)=Z(673,1)*(1.&[1.-Y{674}]*[{Y(248)-Z(248,1)}/Z{248,1}])
Y(674)=X(674)&Z(674,1)
Y(675)=(Y[673]/Y[623])*(Y[335]/Y[297])
Y(676)=(Y[248]*Y[335]/Y[297])/Y(675)
Y(578)=Z(578,1)*(Y[676]/Z[676,1])
Y(588)=Z(588,1)*(Y[676]/Z[676,1])
Y(598)=Z(598,1)*(Y[676]/Z[676,1])
Y(608)=Z(608,1)*(Y[676]/Z[676,1])
Y(637)=Z(637,1)*Y(277)
Y(638)=Z(638,1)*Y(277)
Y(639)=Z(639,1)*Y(277)
Y(640)=(Y[248]*Y[335]/Y[297]-Y[637]/[1.0E&6]*Y[578]-Y[638]/
        [1.0E&6]*Y[588]-Y[639]/[1.0E&6]*Y[598])/Y(608)*(1.0E&6)
Y(677)=Z(677,1)*(1.&[1.-Y{678}]*[{(254)-Z(254,1)}/Z{254,1}])
Y(678)=X(678)&Z(678,1)
Y(679)=(Y[677]/Y[623])*(Y[334]/Y[297])
Y(680)=(Y[254]*Y[334]/Y[297])/Y(679)
Y(579)=Z(579,1)*(Y[680]/Z[680,1])
Y(589)=Z(589,1)*(Y[680]/Z[680,1])
Y(599)=Z(599,1)*(Y[680]/Z[680,1])
Y(609)=Z(609,1)*(Y[680]/Z[680,1])
Y(641)=Z(641,1)*Y(277)
Y(642)=Z(642,1)*Y(277)
Y(643)=Z(643,1)*Y(277)
Y(644)=(Y[254]*Y[334]/Y[297]-Y[641]/[1.0E&6]*Y[579]-Y[642]/
        [1.0E&6]*Y[589]-Y[643]/[1.0E&6]*Y[599])/Y(609)*(1.0E&6)
Y(681)=Z(681,1)*(1.&[1.-Y{682}]*[{Y(251)-Z(251,1)}/Z{251,1}])
Y(682)=X(682)&Z(682,1)
Y(683)=(Y[681]/Y[623])*(Y[336]/Y[297])
```

```
Y(684)=(Y[251]*Y[336]/Y[297])/Y(683)
Y(580)=Z(580,1)*(Y[684]/Z[684,1])
Y(590)=Z(590,1)*(Y[684]/Z[684,1])
Y(600)=Z(600,1)*(Y[684]/Z[684,1])
Y(610)=Z(610,1)*(Y[684]/Z[684,1])
Y(645)=Z(645,1)*Y(277)
Y(646)=Z(646,1)*Y(277)
Y(647)=Z(647,1)*Y(277)
Y(648)=(Y[251]*Y[336]/Y[297]-Y[645]/[1.0E&6]*Y[580]-Y[646]/
         [1.0E&6]*Y[590]-Y[647]/[1.0E&6]*Y[600])/Y(610)*(1.0E&6)
Y(685)=Z(685,1)*(1.&[1.-Y{686}]*[{Y(252)-Z(252,1)}/Z{252,1}])
Y(686)=X(686)&Z(686,1)
Y(687)=(Y[685]/Y[623])*(Y[337]-Y[297])
Y(688)=(Y[252]*Y[337]/Y[297])/Y(687)
Y(581)=Z(581,1)*(Y[688]/Z[688,1])
Y(591)=Z(591,1)*(Y[688]/Z[688,1])
Y(601)=Z(601,1)*(Y[688]/Z[688,1])
Y(611)=Z(611,1)*(Y[688]/Z[688,1])
Y(649)=Z(649,1)*Y(277)
Y(650)=Z(650,1)*Y(277)
Y(651)=Z(651,1)*(Y[687]/Z[687,1])
Y(652)=(Y[252]*Y[337]/Y[297]-Y[649]/[1.0E&6]*Y[581]-Y[650]/
         [1.0E&6]*Y[591]-Y[651]/[1.0E&6]*Y[601])/Y(611)*(1.0E&6)
Y(689)=Z(689,1)*(1.&[1.-Y{690}]*[{Y(253)-Z(253,1)}/Z{253,1}])
Y(690)=X(690)&Z(690,1)
Y(691)=(Y[689]/Y[623])*(Y[337]/Y[297])
Y(692)=(Y[253]*Y[337]/Y[297])/Y(691)
Y(582)=Z(582,1)*(Y[692]/Z[692,1])
Y(592)=Z(592,1)*(Y[692]/Z[692,1])
Y(602)=Z(602,1)*(Y[692]/Z[692,1])
Y(612)=Z(612,1)*(Y[692]/Z[692,1])
Y(653)=Z(653,1)*Y(277)
Y(654)-Z(654,1)*Y(277)
Y(655)=Z(655,1)*(Y[691]/Z[691,1])
Y(656)=(Y[253]*Y[337]/Y[297]-Y[653]/[1.0E&6]*Y[582]-Y[654]/
         [1.0E&6]*Y[592]-Y[655]/[1.0E&6]*Y[602])/Y(612)*(1.0E&6)
Y(228)=Z(228,1)*(1.&[1.-Y{693}]*[{(538)-Z(538,1)}/Z{538,1}])
Y(693)=X(693)&Z(693,1)
Y(229)=(Y[228]/Y[623])*(Y[337]/Y[297])
Y(700)=(Y[538]*Y[337]/Y[297])/Y(229)
  If(Y[532].LT.0.0)Y(700)=Z(700,1)&Z(532,1)*Y(623)
Y(583)=Z(583,1)*(Y[700]/Z[700,1])
Y(593)=Z(593,1)*(Y[700]/Z[700,1])
Y(603)=Z(603,1)*(Y[700]/Z[700,1])
Y(613)=Z(613,1)*(Y[700]/Z[700,1])
```

```
Y(657)=Z(657,1)*Y(277)
Y(658)=Z(658,1)*Y(277)
Y(659)=Z(659,1)*(Y[229]/Z[229,1])
Y(660)=(Y[538]*Y[337]/Y[297]-Y[657]/[1.0E&6]*Y[583]-Y[658]/
        [1.0E&6]*Y[593]-Y[659]/[1.0E&6]*Y[603])/Y(613)*(1.0E&6)
Y(230)=Z(230,1)*(1.&[1.-Y{696}]*[{Y(250)-Z(250,1)}/Z{250,1}])
Y(696)=X(696)&Z(696,1)
Y(231)=(Y[230]/Y[623])*(Y[337]/Y[297])
Y(533)=(Y[250]*Y[337]/Y[297])/Y(231)
Y(584)=Z(584,1)*(Y[533]/Z[533,1])
Y(594)=Z(594,1)*(Y[533]/Z[533,1])
Y(604)=Z(604,1)*(Y[533]/Z[533,1])
Y(614)=Z(614,1)*(Y[533]/Z[533,1])
Y(661)=Z(661,1)*Y(277)
Y(662)=Z(662,1)*Y(277)
Y(663)=Z(663,1)*(Y[231]/Z[231,1])
Y(664)=(Y[250]*Y[337]/Y[297]-Y[661]/[1.0E&6]*Y[584]-Y[662]/
        [1.0E&6]*Y[594]-Y[663]/[1.0E&6]*Y[604])/Y(614)*(1.0E&6)
```

200 continue

```
Y(695)=X(695)*.73
Y(233)=(Y[272]*40.)/Y(623)
Y(236)=0.02*Y(695)
Y(694)=(Y[695]-[Y{624}&Y{668}&Y{672}&Y{676}&Y{680}&
        Y{684}&Y{688}&Y{692}&Y{533}&Y{700}]/Y[623])-
        Y(532)-Y(233)-Y(236)
Y(530)=Y(532)/Y(695)
Y(501)=Y(501)&Y(694)
  If(ITT.EQ.1)Y(501)=0.0
```

Savings Block

```
Y(528)=Z(528,2)&(Z[619,1]*Z[571,1]/[1.0E&6])*Z(567,1)
Y(529)=Z(529,2)&(Z[257,1]*Z[572,1]/[1.0E&6])*Z(568,1)
Y(531)=Z(531,2)&(Z[258,1]*Z[573,1]/[1.0E&6])*Z(569,1)
Y(1)=Z(1,1)
Y(556)=Y(575)*Y(625)/(1.0E&6)&Y(576)*Y(629)/(1.0E&6)&
        Y(577)*Y(633)/(1.0E&6)&Y(578)*Y(637)/(1.0E&6)&
        Y(579)*Y(641)/(1.0E&6)&Y(580)*Y(645)/(1.0E&6)&
        Y(581)*Y(649)/(1.0E&6)&Y(582)*Y(653)/(1.0E&6)&
        Y(583)*Y(657)/(1.0E&6)&Y(584)*Y(661)/(1.0E&6)&
        Y(267)&Y(528)*.07&(Z(559,1)&Z(562,1))*Y(1)&
        (Z[565,1]-Z[565,2])*.10
Y(559)=Y(585)*Y(626)/(1.0E&6)&Y(586)*Y(630)/(1.0E&6)&
        Y(587)*Y(634)/(1.0E&6)&Y(588)*Y(638)/(1.0E&6)&
        Y(589)*Y(642)/(1.0E&6)&Y(590)*Y(646)/(1.0E&6)&
```

```
          Y(591)*Y(650)/(1.0E&6)&Y(592)*Y(654)/(1.0E&6)&
          Y(593)*Y(658)/(1.0E&6)&Y(594)*Y(662)/(1.0E&6)&
          Y(272)&Y(529)*.07-Z(559,1)*Y(1)&(Z[565,1]-Z[565,2])*.10
Y(562)=Y(595)*Y(627)/(1.0E&6)&Y(596)*Y(631)/(1.0E&6)&
          Y(597)*Y(635)/(1.0E&6)&Y(598)*Y(639)/(1.0E&6)&
          Y(599)*Y(643)/(1.0E&6)&Y(600)*Y(647)/(1.0E&6)&
          Y(601)*Y(651)/(1.0E&6)&Y(602)*Y(655)/(1.0E&6)&
          Y(603)*Y(659)/(1.0E&6)&Y(604)*Y(663)/(1.0E&6)&
          Y(531)*.07-Z(562,1)*Y(1)&(Z[565,1]-Z[565,2])*.10
Y(565)=([Y{215}-Y{536}-Y{320}&Y{405}&Y{321}]/Y[297])-
          Y(556)-Y(559)-Y(562)-(Z[565,1]-Z[565,2])*.30
Y(412)=Z(550,1)&Z(551,1)&Z(552,1)&Z(553,1)
Y(347)=Z(347,1)*1.1
Y(348)=Z(348,1)*1.1
Y(349)=Z(349,1)*1.1
Y(555)=Y(556)-(Y[318]*Z[550,1]/Y[412])&Y(347)
Y(558)=Y(559)-(Y[318]*Z[551,1]/Y[412])&Y(348)
Y(561)=Y(562)-(Y[318]*Z[552,1]/Y[412])&Y(349)
Y(564)=Y(565)-(Y[318]*Z[553,1]/Y[412])-Y(292)
Y(557)=Y(318)*Z(550,1)/Y(412)
Y(560)=Y(318)*Z(551,1)/Y(412)
Y(563)=Y(318)*Z(552,1)/Y(412)
Y(566)=Y(318)*Z(553,1)/Y(412)
Y(243)=40.*Y(272)
Y(244)=0.02*Y(695)*Y(623)
Y(245)=Y(532)*Y(623)
Y(571)=Y(575)&Y(576)&Y(577)&Y(578)&Y(579)&Y(580)&Y(581)&
          Y(582)&Y(583)&Y(584)&Y(245)
Y(572)=Y(585)&Y(586)&Y(587)&Y(588)&Y(589)&Y(590)&Y(591)&
          Y(592)&Y(593)&Y(594)&Y(243)
Y(573)=Y(595)&Y(596)&Y(597)&Y(598)&Y(599)&Y(600)&Y(601)&
          Y(602)&Y(603)&Y(604)
Y(574)=Y(605)&Y(606)&Y(607)&Y(608)&Y(609)&Y(610)&Y(611)&
          Y(612)&Y(613)&Y(614)&Y(244)
Y(567)=(Y[555]/Y[571])*(1.0E&6)
Y(420)=([Y{567}/16600.]-1.)*.15
  If(Y[420].NE..0)Y(420)=X(420)
  If(X[420].EQ.1.)Y(420)=0.
Y(568)=(Y[558]/Y[572])*(1.0E&6)
Y(569)=(Y[561]/Y[573])*(1.0E&6)
Y(570)=(Y[564]/Y[574])*(1.0E&6)
Y(619)=([Y{567}/40000.]/100.)*(Y[278]*.5&1.)
  If(Z[429,1].GT.0.2)Y(619)=([Y{567}/50000./100.]*[Y{278}*.5&1.])
Y(619)=Y(619)*1.2
Y(615)=Y(567)*(1.-Y[619])
```

```
Y(257)=([Y{568}/40000.]/100.)*(Y[278]*.5&1.)
  If(Z[429,1].GT.0.2)Y(257)=([Y{568}/50000./100.]*[Y{278}*.5&1.])
Y(257)=Y(257)*1.2
Y(616)=Y(568)*(1.-Y[257])
Y(258)=([Y{569}/40000.]/100.)*(Y[278]*.5&1.)
  If(Y[258].GT.0.10)Y(258)=0.10
  If(Z[429,1].GT.0.2)Y(258)=([Y{569}/50000./100.]*[Y{278}*.5&1.])
Y(258)=Y(258)*1.2
Y(617)=Y(569)*(1.-Y[258])
Y(259)=([Y{570}/40000.]/100.)*(Y[278]*.5&1.)
  If(Y[259].GT.0.10)Y(259)=0.10
  If(Z[429,1].GT.0.2)Y(259)=([Y{570}/50000./100.]*[Y{278}*.5&1.])
Y(618)=Y(570)*(1.-Y[259])
Y(550)=(Y[615]/[1.0E&6])*Y(571)
Y(551)=(Y[616]/[1.0E&6])*Y(572)
Y(552)=(Y[617]/[1.0E&6])*Y(573)
Y(553)=(Y[618]/[1.0E&6])*Y(574)
Y(554)=Y(550)&Y(551)&Y(552)&Y(553)
Y(535)=Y(320)-Y(434)
Y(327)=Y(215)-Y(536)-Y(320)&Y(405)-Y(554)*Y(304)&Y(321)
Y(536)=Y(380)*Y(297)
Y(301)=Y(327)&Y(535)&Y(536)
Y(290)=X(290)
Y(86)=X(86)
Y(421)=Y(480)&Y(86)-Y(423)
  If(Y[195].EQ.2000.)Y(421)=0.
Y(300)=.415*Z(494,1)
Y(305)=Y(301)&Y(303)
```

Expenditure Block

```
Y(207)=Z(207,1)*(1.&1.75*[{Y(615)-Z(615,1)}/Z{615,1}])
Y(208)=Z(208,1)*(1.&1.44*[{Y(616)-Z(616,1)}/Z{616,1}])
Y(209)=Z(209,1)*(1.&1.13*[{Y(617)-Z(617,1)}/Z{617,1}])
Y(210)=Z(210,1)*(1.&.725*[{Y(618)-Z(618,1)}/Z{618,1}])
Y(201)=Y(207)*Y(571)/(1.0E&6)&Y(208)*Y(572)/(1.0E&6)&
          Y(209)*Y(573)/(1.0E&6)&Y(210)*Y(574)/(1.0E&6)
Y(211)=Z(211,1)*(1.&3.00*[{Y(615)-Z(615,1)}/Z{615,1}])
Y(214)=Z(214,1)*(1.&2.38*[{Y(616)-Z(616,1)}/Z{616,1}])
Y(216)=Z(216,1)*(1.&1.86*[{Y(617)-Z(617,1)}/Z{617,1}])
Y(217)=Z(217,1)*(1.&1.29*[{Y(618)-Z(618,1)}/Z{618,1}])
Y(202)=Y(211)*Y(571)/(1.0E&6)&Y(214)*Y(572)/(1.0E&6)&
          Y(216)*Y(573)/(1.0E&6)&Y(217)*Y(574)/(1.0E&6)
Y(218)=Z(218,1)*(1.&1.04*[{Y(615)-Z(615,1)}/Z{615,1}])
Y(219)=Z(219,1)*(1.&1.06*[{Y(616)-Z(616,1)}/Z{616,1}])
Y(220)=Z(220,1)*(1.&1.11*[{Y(617)-Z(617,1)}/Z{617,1}])
```

```
Y(221)=Z(221,1)*(1.&1.12*[{Y(618)-Z(618,1)}/Z{618,1}])
Y(222)=Y(218)*Y(571)/(1.0E&6)&Y(219)*Y(572)/(1.0E&6)&
       Y(220)*Y(573)/(1.0E&6)&Y(221)*Y(574)/(1.0E&6)
Y(223)=Z(223,1)*(1.&1.81*[{Y(615)-Z(615,1)}/Z{615,1}])
Y(224)=Z(224,1)*(1.&.717*[{Y(616)-Z(616,1)}/Z{616,1}])
Y(225)=Z(225,1)*(1.&.447*[{Y(617)-Z(617,1)}/Z{617,1}])
Y(226)=Z(226,1)*(1.-.140*[{Y(618)-Z(618,1)}/Z{618,1}])
Y(227)=Y(223)*Y(571)/(1.0E&6)&Y(224)*Y(572)/(1.0E&6)&
       Y(225)*Y(573)/(1.0E&6)&Y(226)*Y(574)/(1.0E&6)
```

Investment Block (1973 Constant)

```
Y(503)=(Y[324]-Z[324,1])*Y(401)
Y(504)=(Y[206]-Z[206,1])*Y(402)
Y(505)=(Y[205]-Z[205,1])*0.57
  If(Y[195].GE.1980.)Y(505)=(Y[205]-Z[205,1])*.75
  If(Y[195].GT.1990.)Y(505)=(Y[205]-Z[205,1])*1.0
Y(506)=(Y[203]-Z[203,1])*Y(403)
Y(507)=([Y{513}-Z{513,1}]/[1.0E&4])*12.*415.
Y(508)=(Y[204]-Z[204,1])*Y(404)
Y(309)=Y(503)&Y(504)&Y(505)&Y(506)&Y(507)&Y(508)
Y(282)=X(282)
  If(ABS[Y{282}].LT.1)Y(282)=Z(282,1)*(1&X[282])
Y(283)-(Y[248]-Z[248,1])*2.&(Y[255]-Z[255,1])*Y(406)
  If(Y[283].LE.Z[283,1])Y(283)=Z(283,1)*([Y{248}-Z{248,1}]/
                                 Z[248,1])&Z(283,1)
Y(284)=(Y[250]-Z[250,1])*Y(407)
  If(Y[284].LE.Z(284,1])Y(284)=Z(284,1)*([Y{250}-Z{250,1}]/
                                 Z[250,1])&Z(284,1)
Y(285)=(Y[252]-Z[252,1])*Y(408)
Y(286)=(Y[254]-Z[254.1])*Y(409)
Y(261)=Z(261.1)&X(261)
Y(326)=.33*Y(416)*Y(251)*([{1.&Y(261)}**3.]-1.)
Y(537)=(Y[538]-Z[538,1])*Y(417)
Y(539)=(Y[253]-Z[253,1])*Y(418)
  If(Y[539].LE.Z[539,1])Y(539)=Z(539,1)*([Y{253}-Z{253,1}]/
                                 Z[253,1])&Z(539,1)
Y(380)=.010*Y(268)
Y(288)=(Y[268]-Z[268,1])*.20
Y(549)=(Y[546]-Z[546,1])*Y(419)
Y(306)=Y(305)
Y(280)=Y(301)/Y(334)&Y(303)/(Y[491]*Z[494,1])
Y(425)=Y(280)-Y(282)-Y(283)-Y(284)-Y(285)-Y(286)-Y(309)-
       Y(312)-Y(326)-Y(537)-Y(539)-Y(380)-Y(288)-Y(549)
Y(195)=Z(195,1)&1.0
```

```
Y(541)=.077*Y(425)
  If(Y[195].GT.1984.)Y(541)=.248*Y(425)
Y(543)=.552*Y(425)
  If(Y[195].GT.1984.0)Y(543)=.552*Y(425)
Y(547)=.126*Y(425)
  If(Y[195].GT.1984.)Y(547)=.15*Y(425)
Y(548)=.245*Y(425)
  If(Y[195].GT.1984)Y(548)=.05*Y(425)
Y(242)=Y(541)&Y(543)&Y(547)&Y(548)&Y(549)
Y(287)=Y(280)-Y(380)
```

Domestic consumption

```
Y(487)=Y(215)-Y(301)-Y(317)
```

Rest of Trade Block

```
Y(262)=Z(262,1)*(1.&1.00*[Y{555}&Y{558}&Y{561}-Z{555,1}-
        Z{558,1}-Z{561,1}]/[Z{555,1}&Z{558,1}&Z{561,1}])
Y(263)=Z(263,1)*(1.&1.10*[Y{564}-Z{564,1}]/Z[564,1])
  If(Y[195].GT.1990.0)Y(263)=Z(263,1)*(1.&1.00*[Y{564}-
                              Z{564,1}]/Z[564,1])
Y(249)=Y(262)&Y(263)
Y(353)=Y(249)-(Y[544]&Y[545])*2.
  If(Y[353].LT.0.0)Y(353)=0.0
Y(428)=Y(249)-(Y[544]&Y[545])*2.
  If(Y[428].GT.0.0)Y(428)=0.0
Y(423)=Y(227)-Y(240)*1.03
Y(359)=Y(423)
  If(Y[359].LT.0.)Y(359)=0.
Y(360)=Y(351)&Y(352)&Y(353)&Y(359)&Y(368)
Y(317)=Y(353)*Y(477)
Y(369)=Y(359)*Y(475)
Y(298)=Y(315)&Y(316)&Y(317)&Y(369)&Y(500)
Y(371)=(Y[299]&Y[303]-Y[316]-Y[317]-Y[369]-Y[500])/Y(492)
  If(Y[371].LE.400.)Y(372)=0.0
  If(Y[371].GT.400.)
Y(372)=EXP(-.159&.336*ALOG[Y{241}]&ALOG[Y{297}]-
        .33*ALOG[Y{371}])
Y(361)=Y(303)-(Y[298]-Y[299])
Y(374)=Y(371)*Y(492)
Y(370)=Y(372)/Y(492)
Y(345)=Z(345,1)
Y(346)=Z(346,1)
Y(494)=Z(494,1)
  If(Y[371].GT.400.)Y(494)=Y(370)
Y(414)=Y(299)&Y(303)
Y(373)=Y(371)&Y(352)&Y(353)&Y(359)&Y(368)
```

Y(415)=Y(303)−(Y[414]−Y[299])
Y(699)=Z(699,1)*([{Y(268)−Z(268,1)}/Z{268,1}]*1.05&1.)
Y(426)=Y(315)&Y(316)&Y(317)
Y(357)=Y(699)−Y(542)−Y(204)*.5−Y(371)*.4
Y(429)=Y(357)/Y(699)
Y(430)=−Z(427,1)
Y(431)=−Z(428,1)
Y(432)=Y(430)*Y(436)
Y(442)=Y(431)*(436)

Terms of trade
Y(71)=Y(299)/Y(350)
Y(72)=Y(414)/Y(373)
Y(155)=−Y(350)
Y(156)=Y(299)/Y(72)&Y(155)
Y(154)=Y(71)/Y(72)
Y(157)=Y(155)−Y(156)

Monetary Block

Y(422)=Z(422,1)*(1.&0.73*[{Z(422,1)−Z(422,2)}/Z{422,2}]&
0.539*[{Y(268)−Z(268,1)}/Z{268,1}]−0.52*[{Y(297)−
Z(297,1)}/Z{297,1}])
Y(490)=Y(422)*Y(297)
Y(395)=(Y[490]−Z[490,1])/1.18
Y(396)=Y(395)−Y(322)&Y(320)/Y(297)

Inequality Block

Y(379)=Y(571)&Y(572)&Y(573)&Y(574)
Y(378)=Y(555)&Y(558)&Y(561)&Y(564)
Y(381)=Y(571)/Y(379)
Y(382)=Y(572)/Y(379)
Y(383)=Y(573)/Y(379)
Y(384)=Y(574)/Y(379)
Y(385)=Y(555)/Y(378)
Y(386)=Y(558)/Y(378)
Y(387)=Y(561)/Y(378)
Y(388)=Y(564)/Y(378)
Y(389)=Y(385)
Y(390)=Y(389)&Y(386)
Y(391)=Y(390)&Y(387)
Y(392)=Y(391)&Y(388)
Y(393)=(1.−[Y{381}*Y{389}&Y{382}*{Y(389)&Y(390)}&
Y{383}*{Y(390)&Y(391)}&Y{384}*{Y(391)&Y(392)}])/1.00
Y(520)=([24000./{1.0E&6}]*Y[571])−Y(555)

Y(521)=Y(520)/([24000./{1.0E&6}]*Y[571])

National Accounts Block

Y(488)=Y(373)&Y(157)
Y(311)=X(311)
Y(450)=Y(268)&Y(311)
Y(451)=Y(450)&Y(156)
Y(489)=Y(451)&Y(488)
Y(484)=Y(280)−Y(488)
Y(525)=Y(192)/Y(297)
Y(499)=Y(484)−Y(525)
Y(246)=Y(484)&Y(488)
Y(526)=Y(450)−Y(525)
Y(527)=Y(526)&Y(156)
Y(452)=Y(527)−Y(499)
Y(264)=(Y[299]−Y[270])/(Y[350]−Y[362])
Y(265)=Y(270)/Y(362)
Y(274)=−([Y{493}/Y{477}]−1.)*Y(269)
Y(275)=−([Y{440}/Y{477}]−1.)*Y(273)
Y(269)=−1.*(Y[350]−Y[362])
Y(273)=−Y(362)
Y(276)=(Y[299]−Y[270])/Y(72)&Y(269)
Y(291)=Y(270)/Y(72)&Y(273)
Y(308)=Y(269)−Y(276)
Y(310)=Y(273)−Y(291)
Y(355)=Y(268)−Y(525)
Y(356)=Y(311)
Y(375)=Y(355)&Y(356)
Y(313)=Y(268)&Y(276)
Y(314)=Y(311)&Y(291)
Y(325)=Y(313)&Y(314)
Y(328)=Y(373)&Y(310)&Y(308)
Y(354)=Y(325)&Y(328)
Y(377)=Y(280)−Y(328)
Y(394)=Y(377)−Y(525)
Y(329)=Y(313)−Y(525)
Y(330)=Y(314)
Y(331)=Y(329)&Y(330)
Y(376)=Y(331)−Y(394)

Appendix E

Input and Output Tables

THIS APPENDIX FIRST presents the equations from which the basic parameters are estimated, together with the statistics regarding the goodness of their fit. The tables that follow present the parameters and the abridged results of three alternative simulations under varying assumptions regarding the population growth.

Demand Elasticities for Trade, Transport, Services, and Banking

In the equations that follow, the abbreviations used are TRD, trade; TRP, transport; SER, services; BNK, banking; LOG, log; and GNP, gross national product. Figures in parentheses are *t*-statistics. Adjusted elasticities used in the model are as follows: trade, 1.1; transport, 1.1; services, 1.0; and banking, 1.1. All are related to the goods sector.

Sample period 1960–72

$$\text{TRD73} = \underset{(-7.0898)}{-360.815} + \underset{(21.4882)}{0.2470}\ \text{GNP73}$$

$\bar{R}^2 = 0.9746$; Durbin-Watson statistic $= 1.4556$

$$\text{TRP73} = \underset{(1.339)}{20.957} + \underset{(8.356)}{0.0295}\ \text{GNP73}$$

$\bar{R}^2 = 0.8515$; Durbin-Watson statistic $= 1.4506$

$$\text{SER73} = \underset{(9.012)}{125.354} + \underset{(9.527)}{0.0299}\ \text{GNP73}$$

$\bar{R}^2 = 0.8821$; Durbin-Watson statistic $= 0.3408$

$$\text{BNK73} = \underset{(-5.492)}{-99.48} + \underset{(8.525)}{0.0349}\ \text{GNP73}$$

$\bar{R}^2 = 0.8566$; Durbin-Watson statistic $= 0.5486$

$$\text{LOG TRD73} = \underset{(-9.8243)}{-5.5670} + \underset{(21.3807)}{1.4476}\ \text{LOG GNP73}$$

$\bar{R}^2 = 0.9744$; Durbin-Watson statistic $= 1.7039$

$$\text{LOG TRP73} = \underset{(-2.2227)}{-1.8498} + \underset{(8.2313)}{0.8185}\ \text{LOG GNP73}$$

$\bar{R}^2 = 0.8476$; Durbin-Watson statistic $= 1.3634$

$$\text{LOG SER73} = \underset{(2.2014)}{1.0220} + \underset{(9.7363)}{0.5400}\ \text{LOG GNP73}$$

$\bar{R}^2 = 0.8866$; Durbin-Watson statistic $= 0.3857$

$$\text{LOG BNK73} = \underset{(-5.7413)}{-16.8767} + \underset{(7.0547)}{2.4777}\ \text{LOG GNP73}$$

$\bar{R}^2 = 0.8025$; Durbin-Watson statistic $= 0.7055$

Sample period 1967–72

$$\text{TRD73} = \underset{(-5.1578)}{-504.464} + \underset{(14.1624)}{0.2742}\ \text{GNP73}$$

$\bar{R}^2 = 0.9756$; Durbin-Watson statistic $= 1.9484$

$$\text{TRP73} = \underset{(-0.5884)}{-25.332} + \underset{(4.4925)}{0.0383}\ \text{GNP73}$$

$\bar{R}^2 = 0.7932$; Durbin-Watson statistic $= 1.9410$

$$\text{SER73} = \underset{(48.4864)}{183.624} + \underset{(25.1333)}{0.0188}\ \text{GNP73}$$

$\bar{R}^2 = 0.9921$; Durbin-Watson statistic $= 1.7617$

$$\text{BNK73} = \underset{(-7.9343)}{183.469} + \underset{(11.0927)}{0.0508}\ \text{GNP73}$$

$\bar{R}^2 = 0.9606$; Durbin-Watson statistic $= 2.3656$

$$\text{LOG TRD73} = \underset{(-8.7206)}{-6.5369} + \underset{(17.7271)}{1.5609}\ \text{LOG GNP73}$$

$\bar{R}^2 = 0.9843$; Durbin-Watson statistic $= 2.1885$

$$\text{LOG TRP73} = \underset{(-1.9525)}{-4.1853} + \underset{(4.3341)}{1.0913}\ \text{LOG GNP73}$$

$\bar{R}^2 = 0.7806$; Durbin-Watson statistic $= 1.8012$

$$\text{LOG SER73} = \underset{(16.9273)}{2.7861} + \underset{(17.2631)}{0.3338}\ \text{LOG GNP73}$$

$\bar{R}^2 = 0.9834$; Durbin-Watson statistic $= 1.5270$

$$\text{LOG BNK73} = \underset{(-8.8990)}{-28.7497} + \underset{(10.1850)}{0.3851}\ \text{LOG GNP73}$$

$\bar{R}^2 = 0.9536$; Durbin-Watson statistic $= 2.7127$

Table E1. Interindustrial Relations of the Indonesian Economy, 1969
(Thousand millions of rupiahs)

Originator activities	Destination activities: Food	Other agriculture	Minerals	Manufacturing	Construction	Transport	Other	Total
Food	16,446	5,543	—	391,184	—	7	4,289	417,469
	(0.021)	(0.010)		(0.311)			(0.003)	
Other agriculture	627	40,154	58	185,042	17,733	48	2,803	246,505
	(0.001)	(0.070)		(0.148)	(0.105)		(0.002)	
Minerals	—	181	7,613	48,917	23,026	31	73	79,841
			(0.038)	(0.039)	(0.135)			
Manufacturing	12,509	40,788	8,580	201,700	32,686	56,025	72,420	424,708
	(0.005)	(0.064)	(0.039)	(0.078)	(0.147)	(0.208)	(0.054)	
Construction	—	—	690	—	727	170	4,378	5,965
			(0.003)		(0.004)	(0.001)	(0.003)	
Transport	1,094	5,505	397	13,991	4,388	20,494	38,010	83,879
	(0.001)	(0.010)	(0.002)	(0.011)	(0.026)	(0.077)	(0.028)	
Others	32,365	28,360	17,399	156,708	26,757	49,627	400,952	712,159
	(0.041)	(0.049)	(0.087)	(0.125)	(0.157)	(0.188)	(0.301)	
Total, intermediate outputs	63,032	120,531	34,731	997,542	105,357	126,402	522,925	1,970,526
Noncompetitive imports	8.2	4.0	0.8	106.4	7.7	1.2	0	128.0

— Negligible.

Note: Figures in parentheses are coefficients of gross output.

Source: Based on a 40-sector disaggregated table in Y. Kanekoy and J. Luthan, *The Structure of the Indonesian Economy, 1969* (Kyoto: The Center of Southeast Asian Studies, Kyoto University, 1973).

Table E2. Primary Input Composition of Value Added

Primary inputs	Destination activities: Food	Other agriculture	Minerals	Manu- facturing	Construction	Transport	Other	Total
Total value added	724,860	453,828	164,200	253,188	64,900	137,542	810,666	2,609,184
Total input	787,892	574,359	198,937	1,250,730	170,257	263,944	1,333,591	4,579,710
Wages	32,337	83,005	43,956	98,743	45,337	61,660	222,859	706,828
Nonwages	692,523	370,823	120,244	154,445	19,528	75,882	587,814	1,902,356
Ratio of wages to total input	0.0410	0.1445	0.2210	0.0789	0.2665	0.2336	0.1669	0.1543
Ratio of nonwages to total input	0.8790	0.6455	0.6044	0.1235	0.1747	0.2875	0.4408	0.4154

Source: Same as Table E1.

Table E3. Estimated Parameters of Taxes

	Linear regressions, 1967–73				
	Independent variables[a]				
Dependent variable	Constant	GNP, current	Current value of imports and exports	$\bar{R}^2$	Durbin-Watson statistic
Total income taxes[b]	−15.51 (3.5)	0.222 (18.4)		0.983	1.611
Personal income taxes	−2.29 (1.9)	0.005 (16.1)		0.977	1.372
Corporate[c]	−13.47 (5.2)	0.016 (22.9)		0.989	2.213
Taxes on consumption[d]	−5.76 (1.68)	0.020 (21.2)		0.987	2.259
Sales taxes	−7.26 (2.7)	0.0086 (12.0)		0.960	1.212
Excises	2.02 (.52)	0.0094 (8.9)		0.929	1.107
Taxes on international trade	−10.97 (1.4)	(0.035) (16.9)		0.979	2.509
Import duties[e]	−4.82 (.93)	0.026 (18.5)		0.983	2.480
Export duties	−6.15 (.97)	0.0091 (5.3)		0.820	1.369
Nontax revenue	−6.36 (2.5)	0.0051 (7.4)		0.900	1.329
Total tax[f]	−32.24 (2.8)	0.076 (24.4)		0.990	2.170
Import duties[g]	−7.994 (739)		0.144 (7.735)	0.907	2.266
Export duties	−3.959 (1.156)		0.055 (9.408)	0.936	2.266

Source: World Bank estimates.
a. Figures in parentheses are *t*-statistics.
b. Oil corporation excluded.
c. Plus withholding taxes.

	Logarithmic regressions, 1967–73				
	Independent variables [a]				
Dependent variable	Constant	GNP, current	Current value of imports and exports	$\bar{R}^2$	Durbin-Watson statistic
Total income taxes [b]	−6.60	1.30		0.991	2.463
	(16.0)	(25.2)			
Personal income taxes	−65.44	1.14		0.986	1.868
	(14.8)	(20.6)			
Corporate [c]	−9.10	1.57		0.992	1.983
	(19.4)	(26.7)			
Taxes on consumption [d]	−5.07	1.13		0.985	2.438
	(11.2)	(19.9)			
Sales taxes	−7.05	1.24		0.966	1.693
	(9.3)	(13.1)			
Excises	−5.40	1.10		0.962	1.44
	(7.6)	(12.4)			
Taxes on international trade	−3.65	1.02	1.02	0.981	2.051
	(7.9)	(17.7)	(17.7)		
Import duties [e]	−4.66	1.11		0.988	1.943
	(11.7)	(22.3)			
Export duties	−3.63	0.829		0.492	1.402
	(1.4)	(2.6)			
Nontax revenue	−10.43	1.55		0.788	2.017
	(4.1)	(4.3)			
Total tax [f]	3.67	1.11		0.989	2.079
	(9.5)	(23.1)			
Import duties [g]	−2.885		1.166	0.829	1.016
	(2.219)		(5.479)		
Export duties	−3.709		1.098	0.761	2.078
	(2.478)		(4.48)		

d. Other oil revenue excluded.
e. Plus sales taxes on imports.
f. Excluding oil corporation and other oil revenue.
g. Plus sales taxes on imports.

Table E4. Estimates of Expenditure Elasticities, Rural and Urban Areas, 1969
(Elasticities double log term)

Commodity	*Elasticity, urban and rural*	$\bar{R}^2$	*Elasticity, urban*	$\bar{R}^2$	*Elasticity, rural*	$\bar{R}^2$
Cereal and cassava	0.6138	0.9998	0.4461	0.9997	0.6647	0.9998
Rice	0.6838	0.9983	0.4468	0.9992	0.6690	0.99
Income class 1 [a]	1.81					
Income class 2 [a]	0.717					
Income class 3 [a]	0.447					
Income class 4 [a]	−0.14					
Seafood	1.3263	0.9997	1.2002	0.9990	1.3856	0.9997
Fish	1.3363	0.9998				
Income class 1 [a]	1.75					
Income class 2 [a]	1.99					
Income class 3 [a]	1.13					
Income class 4 [a]	0.725					
Meat	2.1788	0.9939	2.2289	0.9951	2.2724	0.9973
Income class 1	3.0					
Income class 2	2.38					
Income class 3	1.86					
Income class 4	1.29					
Eggs and milk	2.1469	0.9948	2.2949	0.9910	2.0274	0.9980
Vegetables	0.8133	0.9997	0.8958	0.9996	0.8037	0.9997
Fruit and spices	1.4108	0.9976	1.4291	0.9991	1.4115	0.9999
Vegetables and fruits	1.08	0.9923				
Income class 1	1.04					
Income class 2	1.06					
Income class 3	1.11					
Income class 4	1.12					
Alcohol and tobacco	1.1704	0.9999	1.1858	0.9990	1.1850	0.9999
Other foods	1.1287	0.9998	1.0853	0.9998	1.1577	0.9997
Total food	0.9476	0.9999	0.9248	0.9999	0.9587	0.9999
Utilities	0.9194	0.9998	0.9549	0.9996	0.8702	0.9998
Miscellaneous	1.5978	0.9995	1.5468	0.9987	1.4911	0.9991
Clothes and other wearables	1.1415	0.9998	1.0797	0.9995	1.1408	0.9999
Durables	1.7650	0.9990	1.8918	0.9944	1.8527	0.9992
Other expenditures	1.1022	0.999	1.1779	0.9984	1.1444	0.9994

Note: Blank cells indicate that the elasticity was estimated graphically and therefore no statistic is available.

Source: N. Kakwani, "On the Estimation of Engel Elasticities from Grouped Observations with Application to Indonesian Data," World Bank Working Paper (restricted circulation document), July 26, 1975.

a. The four income classes correspond to monthly per capita incomes of Rp. 0-1,000, Rp. 1,000-2,000, Rp. 2,000-4,000, and Rp. 4,000 and above, at 1969 prices.

Table E5. Estimates of Employment Elasticity, 1971–73

Sector	1971: Employment (thousands of workers) (1)	1971: GDP (thousand millions of rupiahs, 1960 prices) (2)	1973: Employment (thousands of workers) (3)	1973: GDP (thousand millions of rupiahs, 1960 prices) (4)	Column (4) ÷ column (3) (rupiahs) (5)	Percentage growth rate, 1971–73: Employment (6)	Percentage growth rate, 1971–73: GDP (7)	Elasticity: 1971–73 (8)	Elasticity: 1974–79 (9)	Elasticity: Used in the model (10)
Agriculture	24,772	280,500	25,218	303,400	12,031	0.9	3.8	0.2	0.2	0.2
Mining	90	34,000	91	49,800	547,253	2.2	21.5	0.1	0.2	0.1
Manufacturing and electricity		56,700		67,300	21,689	2.2	5.9	0.4	0.5	0.4
Large scale	999	41,200	1,068	51,000	46,070	3.3	7.1	0.5	0.5	3.5
Small scale	1,933		1,996	16,300	8,166	1.0	2.5	0.4	0.5	0.6
Construction	737	17,100	1,026	26,400	25,731	17.9	25.5	0.7	0.6	0.6
Trade	3,208	108,500	3,538	137,700	38,920	5.0	12.5	0.4	0.5	0.5
Transport	916	22,100	997	27,300	27,382	4.3	10.8	0.4	0.4	0.4
Services	5.160	31,700	5,732	95,300	2,313	5.3	4.5	1.2	0.6	0.5
Total or average	39,210	608,900	41,203	707,200	17,164	2.5	7.7	0.32	0.37	0.30

Source: World Bank estimates.

Table E6. Total and Working-Age Population under Alternative XI(a) (Low Mortality–Low Fertility), Yearly, 1971–97

Year	Population (thousands) Total	Working age[a]	Ratio of working-age to total population
1971	120,709	60,901	0.505
1972	123,738	62,370	0.504
1973	126,793	63,936	0.504
1974	129,892	65,590	0.505
1975	133,050	67,315	0.506
1976	136,272	69,102	0.507
1977	139,567	70,958	0.508
1978	142,892	72,883	0.510
1979	146,257	74,873	0.512
1980	149,670	76,921	0.514
1981	153,138	79,021	0.516
1982	156,664	81,167	0.518
1983	160,206	83,358	0.520
1984	163,768	85,580	0.523
1985	167,343	87,787	0.524
1986	170,931	89,822	0.525
1987	174,523	92,155	0.528
1988	178,109	94,519	0.531
1989	181,679	96,920	0.533
1990	185,228	99,371	0.536
1991	188,744	101,880	0.540
1992	192,214	104,454	0.543
1993	195,686	107,057	0.547
1994	199,153	109,698	0.551
1995	202,607	112,389	0.555
1996	206,033	115,133	0.559
1997	209,428	117,932	0.563

Source: World Bank estimates.

a. Working age is defined as 15-64 years for males, 15-49 years for females.
b. Under this alternative the following assumptions obtain:

Female life expectancy	*1971*	*1986*	*1997*
Java	49.3	55.5	61.2
Other islands	46.5	53.2	59.2
Children per woman			
Java	5.1	3.7	2.3
Other islands	6.2	4.9	2.9

Table E7. Total and Working-Age Population under Alternative XI(b) (High Mortality–High Fertility), Yearly, 1971–97

Year	*Population (thousands)*		*Ratio of working-age to total population*
	Total	*Working age* [a]	
1971	120,709	60,901	0.505
1972	123,733	62,370	0.504
1973	126,799	63,936	0.504
1974	129,909	65,590	0.505
1975	133,078	67,314	0.506
1976	136,312	69,099	0.507
1977	136,619	70,951	0.508
1978	142,987	72,871	0.510
1979	146,418	74,854	0.511
1980	149,932	76,891	0.513
1981	153,517	78,975	0.514
1982	157,187	81,102	0.516
1983	160,940	83,269	0.517
1984	164,782	85,463	0.519
1985	168,716	87,635	0.519
1986	172,738	89,632	0.519
1987	176,846	91,919	0.519
1988	181,035	94,232	0.521
1989	185,301	96,583	0.521
1990	189,643	98,978	0.522
1991	194,058	101,427	0.523
1992	198,539	103,939	0.524
1993	203,088	106,502	0.524
1994	207,698	109,126	0.525
1995	212,366	111,819	0.527
1996	217,087	114,590	0.528
1997	221,859	117,446	0.529

Source: World Bank estimates.

a. Working age is defined as 15-64 years for males, 15-49 years for females.

b. Under this alternative the following assumptions obtain:

Female life expectancy	*1971*	*1986*	*1997*
Java	49.3	58.1	64.9
Other islands	46.5	54.8	62.6
Children per woman			
Java	5.1	4.3	3.4
Other islands	6.2	5.4	4.5

Table E8. Total and Working-Age Population under Alternative XI(c) (Low Mortality–High Fertility), Yearly, 1971–97

Year	Population (thousands) Total	Working age [a]	Ratio of working-age to total population
1971	120,709	60,901	0.505
1972	123,733	62,370	0.504
1973	126,799	63,936	0.504
1974	129,909	65,590	0.505
1975	133,084	67,315	0.506
1976	136,323	69,103	0.507
1977	139,651	70,958	0.508
1978	143,041	72,883	0.510
1979	146,505	74,873	0.511
1980	150,055	76,921	0.513
1981	153,699	79,021	0.514
1982	157,442	81,167	0.516
1983	161,287	83,358	0.517
1984	165,238	85,580	0.518
1985	169,297	87,787	0.519
1986	173,468	89,822	0.518
1987	177,746	92,155	0.518
1988	182,129	94,523	0.519
1989	186,613	96,935	0.519
1990	191,198	99,402	0.520
1991	195,880	101,931	0.520
1992	200,651	104,532	0.521
1993	205,508	107,193	0.522
1994	210,447	109,926	0.522
1995	215,466	112,745	0.523
1996	220,562	115,655	0.524
1997	225,719	118,661	0.526

Source: World Bank estimates.

a. Working age is defined as 15-64 years for males, 15-49 years for females.
b. Under this alternative the following assumptions obtain:

	1971	1986	1997
Female life expectancy			
Java	49.3	55.5	61.2
Other islands	46.5	53.2	59.2
Children per woman			
Java	5.1	4.3	3.4
Other islands	6.2	5.4	4.5

Table E9. Principal Macroeconomic Indicators under Alternative XI(a) (Low Mortality–Low Fertility)

Indicator	1974	1985	1997	Average annual growth rate 1974–85	Average annual growth rate 1985–97
GDP (at constant price, thousand millions of rupiahs)	6,690	17,149	49,557	8.9	9.3
Population (thousands)	129,892	167,343	209,428	2.4	1.9
Working population (thousands)	47,880	64,083	86,090	2.7	2.5
Unemployment (percent)	6.8	3.6	0		
Gini coefficient	0.422	0.545	0.561		
Poverty index	0.583	0.503	0.168		
Value-added goods sector (billions of rupiahs)	3,732	9,211	25,888	8.6	9.0
Price index (1973=1.00)	1.453	3.785	6.191	9.1	4.6
Nominal exchange rates	415	461	470		
Real wage index (1973=1.00)	1.007	1.009	1.036		
Incremental capital-output ratio				3.23	3.44
Incremental labor-output ratio				1.67	0.750
Foreign saving as percentage of export (current)	18.3	13.5	4.2		
Investment as percentage of GDP (constant)	21.3	27.9	33.5		
Government saving as percentage of GDP (current)	6.9	12.8	16.1		

Source: Macromodel simulation results.

Table E10. Principal Macroeconomic Indicators under Alternative XI(b) (High Mortality–High Fertility)

				Average annual growth rate	
Indicator	*1974*	*1985*	*1997*	*1974–85*	*1985–97*
GDP (at constant price, thousand millions of rupiahs)	6,690	17,120	49,087	8.9	9.2
Population (thousands)	129,909	168,716	221,859	2.4	2.3
Working population (thousands)	47,881	63,974	85,736	2.7	2.5
Unemployment (percent)	6.8	3.5	0		
Gini coefficient	0.422	0.543	0.554		
Poverty index	0.583	0.500	0.169		
Value-added goods sector (billions of rupiahs)	3,732	9,196	25,654	8.5	8.9
Price index (1973=1.00)	1.453	3.790	6.293	9.1	4.3
Nominal exchange rates	415	494	483		
Real wage index (1973=1.00)	980	1.009	1.036		
Incremental capital-output ratio				3.24	3.43
Incremental labor-output ratio				1.68	0.751
Foreign saving as percentage of export (current)	18.2	13.5	4.2		
Investment as percentage of GDP (constant)	20.2	26.8	32.9		
Government saving as percentage of GDP (current)	.69	12.8	16.4		

Source: Macromodel simulation results.

Table E11. Principal Macroeconomic Indicators under Alternative XI(c) (Low Mortality–High Fertility)

Indicator	*1974*	*1985*	*1997*	*Average annual growth rate* 1974–85	*Average annual growth rate* 1985–97
GDP (at constant price, thousand millions of rupiahs)	6,690	17,135	49,156	8.9	9.2
Population (thousands)	129,909	169,297	225,719	2.5	2.4
Working population (thousands)	47,881	64,085	86,623	2.7	2.6
Unemployment (percent)	6.8	3.7	0.009		
Gini coefficient	0.422	0.544	0.564		
Poverty index	0.583	0.506	0.278		
Value-added goods sector (billions of rupiahs)	3,732	9,203	25,595	8.6	8.9
Price index (1973=1.00)	1.453	3.785	6.092	9.1	4.4
Nominal exchange rates	415	462	465		
Real wage index (1973=1.00)	.980	1.008	1.027		
Incremental capital-output ratio				3.24	3.42
Incremental labor-output ratio				1.66	0.752
Foreign saving as percentage of export (current)	18.3	13.5	4.2		
Investment as percentage of GDP (constant)	21.3	27.8	33.0		
Government saving as percentage of GDP (current)	6.9	12.8	15.9		

Source: Macromodel simulation results.

Bibliography

Aghevli, Bijan B. "Money prices and the balance of payments, Indonesia, 1968–73." (Forthcoming in *Journal of Development Studies*, 1977).

Amartya, Sen. *On Economic Inequality*. London: Oxford University Press, 1972.

Carter, N. G., and Hazel Elkington. "A Handbook of Expected Values of Structural Characteristics." World Bank Staff Working Paper no. 154, June 1973; processed.

Chenery, H. B., and others. *Redistribution with Growth*. London: Oxford University Press, 1974.

Gupta, Syamaprasad. "Alternative Development Strategies of Korea (1976–1990) in an Input-Output Dynamic Simulation Model." World Bank Staff Working Paper no. 250, 1977; processed.

Hickman, B. G., ed. *Econometric Models of Cyclical Behavior*. Proceedings of the National Bureau of Economic Research. New York: Columbia University Press, 1972.

Indonesia, Republic of. "The First Five-Year Development Plan." Jakarta: Department of Information, n.d.

———. "The Second Five-Year Development Plan." Jakarta: Department of Information, n.d.

———. *Pendapatan Nasional Indonesia* (National income of Indonesia), 1960–68 and 1970–74. Jakarta: Central Bureau of Statistics, 1970 and 1975.

———. *Survey Sosial Ekonomi Nasional* (National socioeconomic survey), October 1969–December 1969. Jakarta: Central Bureau of Statistics, 1972.

Kanekoy, Y., and J. Luthan. *The Structure of the Indonesian Economy, 1969*. Kyoto: The Center of Southeast Asian Studies, Kyoto University, 1973.

Kutznets, Simon. "Economic Growth and Income Inequality." *American Economic Review* vol. 45, no. 1 (1955), pp. 1–28.

Lopes, F. L. "Inequality Planning in the Developing Economy." Ph.D. dissertation, Harvard University, 1972.

Paukert, F. "Redistribution of Income Patterns of Consumption and Employment: A Case Study for the Philippines." International Labour Organisation Working Paper, 1974.

Swasono, Sri Edi, Hendra, Esmara, and others. *Perhitungan Pendapatan Regional Di Indonesia* (Regional income in Indonesia, 1968–72). 3 vols. Jakarta: Planning Commission, 1974.